TRANSMAN - BITESIZE

The story of a Woman who became a Man

RICO ADRIAN PARIS

authorHOUSE™

1663 LIBERTY DRIVE, SUITE 200
BLOOMINGTON, INDIANA 47403
(800) 839-8640
WWW.AUTHORHOUSE.COM

First published by AuthorHouse 12/01/05

ISBN: 1-4259-0576-5 (sc)

Printed in the United States of America
Bloomington, Indiana

This book is printed on acid-free paper.

INSPIRED BY MY FATHER WHO died too young, written for my children to help them understand, dedicated to all those men who choose to tread the path I have trodden.

Ivor Leonard Thompson 1923 - 1985
Father and I (aged 5)

Acknowledgments

I WOULD LIKE TO TAKE THIS opportunity to acknowledge and thank the following persons, for their practical help and on-going encouragement in getting this book published:

Jayne Summers

Jenni Peters

Cathy Moss

Antonia and Steve

CONTENTS

TRANSMAN

Introduction

THERE ARE MANY BOOKS IN this world written by ordinary people who live complex lives, you as the reader make the choice for yourself as to which ones you read and why you read them.

You may have stumbled upon this one by chance and are curious to know what it's all about, you may have made an effort to seek it out. It may have been given to you as a gift, or it may have been going cheap at a car boot sale and you like a bargain; who knows. The fact is you've got it, you've read this far, I hope you stick with it.

This book is not meant to be a literary masterpiece, purely my story in my own words. The grammar could probably be better and the words themselves put across in a far more intellectual manner however the language used is the language I know and I did not wish to change any of it.

For my part, as the author, I have wanted for a long time to put pen to paper and start publishing information about my life choices. To raise awareness in the minds of everyday people, anyone with an inquiring mind, on the complex subject of Gender Identity and how it relates to men like myself.

Education is the only way forward for society in general to accept that 'difference' exists in us all. Though that difference can take many forms; colour, race, language, physical ability, age, sexuality, gender, the list is endless. If society will only see, through wide open eyes, we are all the same because we are all different. Every one of us is a unique individual and our differences are the wealth we carry as a species.

For my part, I am a Gender & Sexuality Counsellor who works with transsexual, transgender and transvestite persons in the West Midlands – UK. I am also a Gender & Sexuality Trainer who has written a Trans Awareness Training program for professionals and public service providers that work with, or provide a service to, Trans persons.

In this book, which is the first in a series of three called *'Bite size'* simply because they explore the subject matter in small manageable chunks, you will read about how I went through a transition from female to male. I have included photographs to give depth to the words and a visual experience of my physical change.

You will have access to excerpts from my personal journal which I kept throughout my transition and proved to be an invaluable way of downloading my thoughts, fears and frustrations over what was at times a difficult transition. You will also read how family can react to news of having someone in their midst diagnosed as Trans and a personal viewpoint from, with all things being equal, my wife to be.

I believe it is only by meeting with or reading about persons like myself, that you can gain a real insight into trans and by publishing a book, such as this, that information will continue to be on file for generations to come, available to those who need to educate themselves. Whether they be contemplating making this life choice for themselves or just someone who has, as mentioned earlier, an enquiring mind.

Therein if I am honest, lies the ultimate reason for putting pen to paper and writing this book. By capturing the story of my life choices, tracking the route I have taken, that story remains after I am gone for those that seek to know more about how ordinary men and women live extraordinary lives simple by an error of birth.

TRANSMAN

So What Is Trans?

THERE COULD BE MANY ANSWERS to that question depending upon the context within which the question was first being asked. My analysis of the question comes from a personal view of internal gender identity and external gender expression, coupled with a basic understanding of the medical and academic terminology commonly used.

The subject of 'Trans' has attracted much debate from the powers that be across the world. In an effort to process that debate into some form of understanding of trans, those same powers have tried to sort, shift and file away in their minds and published papers, increasingly more complex information. Unfortunately, in the process, the subject has got tangled up with plenty of terminology leaving your average 'Jo Bloggs' baffled and inquiring minds bogged down with politically correct words which detract from real peoples experience of living with the effects of being trans.

Terminology

I am using the word 'Trans' as a shortened version of Transsexual, the break down of this word and what it represents is described in various ways depending upon which reference material you seek out to clarify the term.

An English Dictionary states: "TRANSSEXUAL a person of one sex who believes his or her true identity is of the opposite sex".

I feel this basic description though true is not that basic at all. When you talk about sex as opposed to gender, when dealing with trans it can be confusing. I would prefer to see something like -'A person who believes their internal gender identity is the direct opposite to their birth gender'. However even that could be incorrect for some people.

Mixing the word sex with gender identity is like walking on thin ice, the word sex pushes a button inside me pertaining to sexual orientation and I don't think I stand alone. For instance a common assumption by society is that a transwoman is in fact a gay man in a dress. For my part when delivering trans awareness training I always distinguish between sex and gender, sexual orientation and gender identity, purely to help students 'sort, shift and file' the correct information.

The Harry Benjamin Standards of Care (produce internationally accepted guidelines for medical professionals dealing with patients exhibiting Gender Identity Disorder) state: "The desire to live and be accepted as a member of the opposite sex, usually accompanied by the wish to make his or her body congruent as possible with the preferred sex through surgery and hormone treatment. The transsexual identity has been present persistently for at least two years. The disorder is not a symptom of another mental disorder or chromosomal abnormality".

It is clearly beneficial to have a plan of action, this is exactly what the standards of care are if you bring them down to basic interpretations, the interesting point I feel is that just how many medical professionals or trans people for that matter, do not know these standards of care exist and would they follow them anyway? Certainly in my experience of working within my local trans community over the past four years, there is a decided lack of knowledge on both sides and I find that troubling.

Gender Identity Research and Education Society (GIRES) GIRES' primary mission is to improve the circumstances in which trans people live, by changing the way that society treats them. Accordingly, its aim is to generate supportive attitudes among all those who can make those improvements happen, including politicians, other policy makers, clinicians and the providers of commercial and government services including the police and teachers, as well as employers, journalists and family members. GIRES' approach is based on research into the origins of atypical gender identity development and transsexualism and, also, into the way that society reacts to the people experiencing these conditions. It develops good practice guidelines, education programmes and literature, all specially tailored for each of the groups that it aims to influence. (Words with kind permission of GIRES). http://www.gires.org.uk

Now I feel that last paragraph was a bit heavy to understand by most and gets even heavier when you listen to or read information which distinguishes transsexualism from intersex conditions.

Intersex, in basic terms, is a word used to describe someone born with ambiguous genitalia or other biological factors which mean a decision has to be made as to what gender or sex that person will be labelled with. I feel that if there is some medical evidence to show there is a biological reason for individuals having gender identity issues then surely transsexualism should also be classed as a type of intersex condition? Just my own opinion but I'm sure one mirrored by many others.

If, after reading the information on terminology which I have kept brief on purpose, you are left with more questions than answers there are a list of reference materials at the end of this publications. I really do not want to mirror in this manuscript work that has been done elsewhere, from a terminological point of view other books, good books, are out there for you to read if you so wish.

At the time of this book going to print there were approximately 60 different trans groups in the U.K. These groups, or service providers, range in size from Registered Charities to local 'lets meet in someone's home' type support. Each provides a valuable service to Trans people and some have been going for over 30 years.

One of the newly emerging organisations is the United Kingdom Trans Alliance (See www.uktransalliance.org.uk). This organization hopes to be an alliance of many UK based organizations, large or small. One of the aims of this group is to agree some kind of consensus on terminology around Trans, no mean feat but necessary for education on Trans. If there is no common understanding of what each term means how can anyone educate themselves, whether they are trans or not.

What is 'trans' to me?

Trans is a word that I have had to learn to accept. It is a word I accept more than transsexual which I struggle to identify with and if those are my two choices of descriptive word to identify me as being born female but identifying as male, I choose trans any day.

Of course I own 'man' for myself without the prefix but people need to box me off into something they can understand or think they understand. So I accept trans in that context. Education is the only way forward in getting the slow grinding machine of society to accept the people who fall outside of the dominant social norm. Which in this country, I believe, even though much work has been done to try and create a society that considers all of its residents as equal to one another, is still white, able bodied, English speaking, heterosexual and male.

One last thought on what trans is to me, I suppose in a nutshell trans is where I want to be. I made a choice to own this for myself, 'transman' as a label feels the closest description I can use to who I am in this life; biologically female internally male. Man of transsexual origin is another term I feel comfortable with.

I know some would say we make no choice, they would argue that we are born this way and so therefore we have no choice in the matter and I am not disputing that statement. However I do feel we can identify as being the way we are but choose not to do anything visible/actively about it, choose not to bring our outside shell through the medical options available to us, in line with our inner gender identity. Thus my reason for saying to identify as transman is a choice I have made for myself, I feel in all honesty it is one of the only real choices I have been able to make for myself and one I have fought hard to take from fantasy to reality.

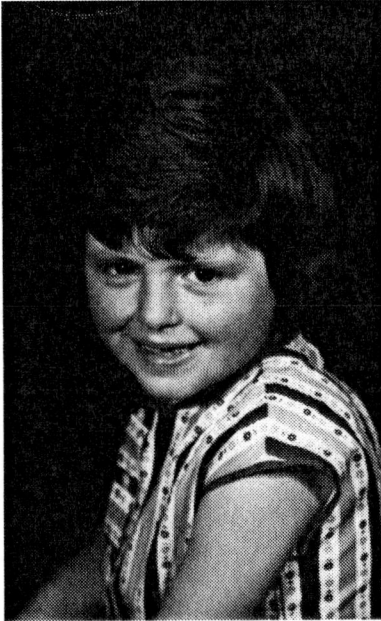

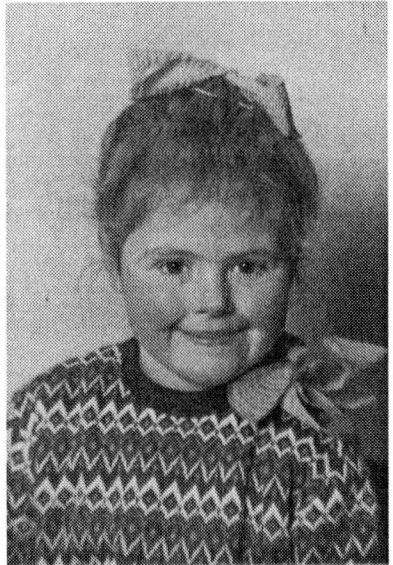

Clockwise from top left; Age 7/8, Age 14, Age 4/5, Age 31

TRANSMAN

History

THE WORD HISTORY PULLS UP in my mind thoughts of Michael Jackson's epic collection of songs and the music video's which bring the songs to life. The word history also brings to mind long, boring lessons at school learning about all sorts of dusty, cobweb covered facts which have brought us into the 21st Century as a race of beings. With those two pictures in mind I will try and make it interesting for you to look at my own history. I feel it is important for you to get some context of how I got into the 21st Century as an individual although 'roots' would be a better description I suppose, yet it is my history so I will stick with that term.

I was born in 1962 at midnight between Halloween and All Saints day, to parents who were in their forties and who did not want, or expect, to find themselves with another child to care for when their life had finally become their own. I believe my parents did their best to provide a happy home for me but things were difficult due to a father who worked hard and drank often and a mother who was very religion focused. My older brother and sister left home by the time I was three years old and so I think it's fair to say I was raised almost as an only child.

The place I grew up in was a little hamlet called Much-Wenlock in Shropshire. My mothers family had lived there for several generations and I was told stories and shown places where our family's presence was still clearly imprinted on the surrounding area. My father, however, and that side of the family came from a little place called Howey outside Llandrindod Wells in Powys, Wales, a place we used to go to at least once a year and filled with fond memories.

One parent English, one parent Welsh, one parent from a wealthy and business minded family and one from a poor 'eke out an existence' sort of background. As a result my childhood was rich with stories of varied cultural challenges, survival in times of hardship and poverty, jack the lad activities and societies best frock parties. Yes my childhood was rich with stories but starved of what really mattered from parents, attention, love, a feeling of being valued as a sibling, in short - quality.

The house I grew up in was a little two up two down end terrace house, one of twelve in a row owned by my Grandfather. He lived at number 1, we lived at number 12 and the ten houses in between granddad rented out to various people, mainly old people with whom I spent many a happy hour visiting and listening to stories of the 'olden days'. I remember in particular old Miss Sandals who was a spinster and retired school teacher. She used to make her own butter and cheese with curds and old stockings in a dark and dingy old kitchen and fed hundreds of wild birds in her garden with a concoction of seeds and lard which was brewed in a battered saucepan and left to set in an old flowerpot. I remember the old dear having no television, only an old radio which played old songs and the tired but clean furniture in her front room draped over with crochet blankets, with church magazines scattered about and fresh flowers from her garden on old shabby sideboards.

I loved to spend time with older people when I was a child, they were fascinating to me. I was drawn to them like a moth to the flame including my own Grandfather who was actually disabled due to a supposed fall off a quarry face on the Windmill Hill – Much Wenlock, in his early 70's. This was the official story I was told as a child but as an adult there was talk of his accident being an attempted suicide from depression.

My Grandfather had no legs, only stumps, with crude prosthetic legs that with the aid of sticks helped him get around a little. Though he mainly lived in his wheel chair, granddad did get about a bit. I remember he also had a metal plate in his skull as a result of the fall. I can recall now how he sat in his wheel chair in the corner of his dimly lit kitchen, light was provided by an old gas lamp and the fireplace. He sat there with a bottle of brown ale delivered to him by davenports or some other delivery firm, a slice of home made bread and a big chunk of cheese, twiddling his thumbs, one round the other and staring at me with a non expressional glare.

I think I was a bit of nuisance to the old guy so grandfather kept giving me things to do to get me out of his way, but I was persistent and I kept coming back. Often his door was locked so I would go and see one of the other old folks in the row instead.

My grandfather died when I was young, grandmother had died when I was about 4, I was about 9 when he died. Yet even after his death I would go and let myself into the empty house and sit for hours feeling somekind of kinship with the place. I felt acutely aware even before the teenage years that my parents were old in my eyes, my last grandparent had died and not many relatives where still knocking around. I felt cheated of the extended family I should have had if only I had been born when my parents were younger. I felt adrift somehow.

I have many vivid memories of childhood as we all do, mine is very much a mixed bag of good times and not so good times. One of my earliest fond memories is sitting on my fathers shoulders looking out across the Dale end in Ironbridge, at a fire engine rushing through the valley towards some emergency somewhere. I could only have been about three years old, a sobering thought to realize our children even that young can recall what happens to them.

Another memory or set of memories I have are around my father calling me 'Boyo' or 'Bonzo', neither name I objected to. What I did object to was getting kicked in the back when my father was sitting in his arm chair and I was sitting on the floor watching TV. I never did understand why he did that, I would look around and his face was full of anger but I had done nothing except sit there and be kicked, if I objected I just got another one so I put up and shut up or went to bed. I think my father was a very angry and confused man, I do know that he was at least bisexual yet had lived a married life with a wife and family and I can't help but wonder if he had been true to himself if life would have been better for him.

Father decided to marry my mother for what ever reason and he should have been content with his choice. The reality was he seemed so unhappy with his lot in life and eventually died at the young age of 61. I had only known him a short 23 years and he never really knew me at all.

My mother was a very religious woman, we attended meetings at least three times a week and I was taught through bible study the rights and wrongs of mankind, our strengths and weaknesses and to look to God for the answer to life's troubles. I was taught that the wrongs of the world in this life would be made right in the new order which was coming soon to engulf the world. A new theocratically governed kingdom which only the pure of heart would inherit was coming and I had to avoid temptation and keep my eyes on the prize to get into this wonderful promised land.

I will not use this space to slate a religion that my mother has given fifty years of her life to however there is no getting a way from the fact, as a child to be so indoctrinated by a devout religion in the way I was produced a very inhibited and narrow minded adult. I had to break down all that I had learned as a child before I could be free to make my own mind up as to what life was all about and where or even if a Deity fitted into the grand scheme of things.

Due to my mothers strong convictions my parents did not celebrate things like birthdays, Easter or Christmas and I have lots of memories around why that was so. I had it explained to me that based on the teachings of Christ it is better to celebrate a persons death than their birth and that Christmas was therefore unacceptable but the memorial of Christ's death was acceptable to celebrate. To be honest though this analogy never really sank in and I came up with all sorts of schemes to try and get recognition for myself on these special days much to my mother's disgust. What child wouldn't wish to be acknowledged on these celebratory days? But my attempts to be recognized always resulted sadly in a real humdinger of a fall-out between my parents and not a happy time at all.

I remember vividly my thirteenth birthday, I used some of my pocket money to buy a cake and some candles and snuck off to my den, an old converted pig sty which my father had put a window in and a lockable door on. Then he gave the key to me to get in to it whenever I wanted to play in at the bottom of the garden.

The den, that pigsty, was my sanctuary, my bolt hole from my parents, a place where I could explore my fantasies of what families should be like and where my imagination grew. It was also the place I had to go to when I practiced playing the violin; the screeching drove my parent's potty. I played the violin for about 2 years.

Getting back to my 13th birthday, I used my pocket money to buy a cake and candles and I sought out the den. Sitting there in the dark, alone and with the candles lit, I sang myself happy birthday. I felt so damn unwanted and worthless and I remember this was the first time I considered running away from home, though I didn't try that one until I was about fifteen.

Reading that last paragraph through it sounds so patronising, however the feelings were very real and writing this I am catapulted right back to that very moment. As an adult I have found it very difficult to celebrate anything, even birthdays, if I am the focal point. Clearly I have left over baggage psychologically from childhood, on not feeling that I am worth that kind of fuss so it is a major personal achievement to be writing a book such as this, which is after all, is about me.

My parents actually split up when I was about ten years old for a couple of years. This was a really mixed up kind of time for me, my father had left after my parents had fought. I saw him creeping past my bedroom door and asked him where he was going, he made some comment about leaving being the best thing to do and I recall asking my father to take me with him but he said my place was with my mother. I felt abandoned by my father to be left with a mother who I couldn't relate to and I felt didn't understand me at all; a person who I felt I was clearly an inconvenience to. After my father left my mother had a gentlemen friend appear on the scene, I remember his name was Neville and although I firmly believe nothing went on between them, because of mothers devout religious and moral beliefs the man in question did want a relationship with my mother and played his cards with me thinking he would get brownie points with her.

This extra attention I received resulted in me getting everything materially I asked for and to be honest what ten year old wouldn't milk that one for all it was worth? But life was still difficult, even though we went out more and had fun times I missed my father's in-put in my life. I would seek out the key to his museum sitting for hours surrounded by World War II memorabilia, badges, toy soldiers and uniforms. These were the only things my father seemed to value and so I valued them also.

My father had his own museum built in our garden housing an impressive collection of military regalia, he being one of the largest private collectors of military regalia in the country. That was my father's safe haven and he spent most of his time in there or the pub to stay out of the family home. I remember he put a baby mini-com system up so that he could ask mother things and she could speak to him through it to save either of them actually talking face to face. At the end of the day mother did not agree with dad's preoccupation with the military because it was in direct conflict to her religion and dad could not agree with her religion because of his own military interest.

When his health eventually failed the collection was auctioned off in Sotheby's in London, a sad time for both of us. He had spent a life time buried in the war inside that museum, a sanctuary from the outside world, after being medically discharged from the Royal Welsh Fusiliers against his will in or around 1949.

It is worth saying that prior to my father's death he did make the choice to join mothers life long religion, which brought them together at last. For me this was a very challenging stage in my life. I could never except that at the end my father bowed to religion when he had been so independent all his life. Clearly in hindsight I can see that the fear of death made my father reflect on his life and he made choices accordingly but at the time this was a real wake up call to me. I was an active member of that religion and instead of strengthening my faith it dashed it to bits, in such a dramatic way that my faith never recovered and I left the religion within a couple of years.

Getting back to mothers male friend; the man who was interested in my mother died in a horrific car accident and the local Shropshire Star newspaper printed graphic pictures and a story on the front page. I had the newspaper thrust into my hands by a friend of my mothers and told to let my mother know as soon as possible. It became my responsibility to break the news, at the around the age of 11, to my mother, who promptly snatched the paper out of my hands and thrust it in to my fathers face. He was sitting in our living room at the time supposedly on an access visit with me but as usual I had been told to 'go out and play' so they could talk.

HOBBY DROVE HIM OUT OF HIS HOME

Mr Len Thompson, with a small part of his giant collection.

Old soldier Len's toy hobby turns into a museum

Old soldier Len Thompson's fascination for military history has grown into a full-time occupation.

For other collectors of military regalia are frequently seeking help and advice from Mr Thompson, whose Shropshire home has its own private museum with over 12,000 exhibits.

"I have been collecting military regalia and model soldiers for 43 years," said Mr Thompson of Much Wenlock, who has 11,000 badges and 5,100 authentic lead model soldiers in his museum.

"We owe our freedom today to the men who wore these badges, and they are part of our country's history so I thought it was about time someone started to keep a record of them for generations to come.

"I'm a member of the Military History Society and the Military Model Makers Society, and we try to swap items among ourselves, which is the only way someone like myself can acquire some of the more rare pieces.

"I also do a lot of repairing and repainting of model soldiers, which is a full-time occupation in itself.

"I have 800 books to refer to for clothing regulations of a particular period, as you have to be very accurate and the experts would soon spot any mistakes," he said.

Another part of his hobby is to identify and authenticate military badges, including helmet plates and cap badges, for collectors.

Mr Thompson, who retired three years ago from his job at Buildwas Power Station, had 12 years of personal experience of Army life — including several years in Africa during which he was sent to hospital 11 times with malaria.

After joining the artillery as a boy soldier, he fought in the jungles of West Africa with the West African Frontier Force and later, as a sergeant, was seconded to the French Foreign Legion in an instructor's post.

19 Aug 1980

Two of the many newspaper clippings I have, recording the developing collection my father amalgamated.

The result of this news breaking was that my father moved back into the family home the next day and life was expected to return to normal, what ever normal was. I had mixed emotions about my father leaving and then mixed emotions about my father returning, I felt guilty that this man friend of mothers, Neville, had died, as I knew he had stopped visiting mother recently as she had been saying I needed my father back. Neville had taken me for a drive, just the two of us, to tell me this himself and all these raging emotions bottled up in me until around the age of 13 went off like a bottle of pop.

I clearly remember having suicidal thoughts for the first time that very day and being distraught out in the street, comforted by my friend Francis, who was even younger than I because as I said previously, mother had told me to go back out to play while she continued to speak to my father.

Eventually at around about 13 or 14, I was sent to see a child psychiatrist called Dr Bennardy, I can remember him now, a typical middle aged, professor type chap who wanted to know all sorts of personal things about me which made me feel uncomfortable, to say the least, especially the questions about sex and sexual activity. Though I am sure he was only doing his job to try and find out if I was sexually active because to be quite frank I was claiming that I was having sex in the local derelict signal box, the local hang out for skiving delinquents in Much Wenlock, even though this was a pack of lies. Dr Bennardy came across as perverted in the way he made intimate inquiries and this feeling will stay in my mind for eternity.

Strangely enough, when I was married with a couple of young children myself, our family unit was referred to a children's psychiatric unit, due to my eldest son having real development problems and guess who we saw? Yep, good old DR Bennardy. I did not like him the first time round and I certainly did not like him the second time round.

The brief account of my early years I have recorded here is only half the story but I feel it gives you the reader enough to get a feel for what life was like for me. It sounds horrendous reading back but there were many good times, as I have mentioned earlier, and rounding it all up I think I could have done a lot worse than have the parents or upbringing that I did

As an adult and a parent, I truly see that we all do our best and I do not believe for one moment my parents are to blame for my trans status. I know there is this vein of thinking that there is a pattern of parental dysfunction associated with transsexualism, it runs along the lines of dysfunctional father, distraught mother equals trans individual. I do think if this was truly the case, rather than around 1 in 5,000 * of the population for male to female (a lot less for female to male) transsexuals in the UK we would have millions! Families are complex, relationships are complex and as a society we keep on pointing the finger back a generation to the parents, clearly my upbringing was not ideal and has shaped who I am considerably. However, I intend to stop pointing that finger right now by taking ownership for my own life choices, proudly taking ownership, in fact I feel it takes something away from me as a free thinking individual to 'blame' my parents, if I blamed them it would feel like I don't have the right to stand up and be counted on my own merits and how can there be any blame when a multitude of others feel like I do, because we know in our hearts we were born this way.

In the years I have been involved with trans individuals, the books I have read, the programmes I have watched on the TV, I notice time and time again that people talk about their first feeling of knowing they were in the wrong body quite young in life.

I wish I could say that was the case for me but I would be lying to you and myself. For me it has been a gradual awakening, a growing self discovery that has its roots in childhood but only in the way that I felt very different to other children, I kept myself to myself, had an overwhelming feeling of not fitting in, more than that even to the point, I would say of 'not wanting to fit it', not wanting to be like everybody else.

My first real experiences of cross gender feelings would have been in my teens and they were in conversations I found myself having with one or two friends. Though I do remember playing 'dress-up' with a friend called Susan and I always insisted on playing 'the man' and even trying to kiss her which she thought was horrible. I could only have been about 5 or 6 years old.

I remember clearly saying to my friends in our early teens that I was born with both sets of genitals and had surgery as a child to correct the abnormalities. This was a total pile of pants but it was nevertheless the story I told people and believed it wholeheartedly almost like I had convinced myself

---

* Trans-Shropshire statistics in their 04 -05 Annual Report.

that this was really true, for many years. One of the most painful things I have ever had to do was first admit that lie to myself because it was getting in the way of discovering who I really was as a person. I couldn't build the foundations of who I am now on lies.

Before I hit adolescence I was what you would call a tomboy, climbing trees, scrumping apples from the Barnardo's boys orchard. I was even the leader of a gang called the Bovver Boy's which we took so seriously at the time and yet on reflection was pitiful. I used to play football with the lad who lived next door, called David, and my friend's brothers Michael and Daniel, though they always stuck me in goal and beat the crap out of me with the ball. I also did the girlie thing to at times, I liked pretty clothes and long hair until mother tricked me and cut it all off whilst I was asleep at the hairdressers. I liked to play house with dolls or rather the long suffering cat 'Ginger' dressed up in baby clothes and pinned down in the pram by a blanket. Poor old cat put up with a lot from me. I liked girls toys and boys toys when I could get my hands on boys toys. I usually swiped a little lorry or battered old car or even an action man once, because my mother wouldn't let me have one of my own, from my friends house where there was four lads at home and toys went missing all the time. All I wanted the damn action man for was to pretend it was having sex with Barbie. As you can see, I had a healthy interest in sex well before my teens.

At one point, when I was about 13 years old and had just started my first job as Saturday girl for Sketchleys dry cleaners in Bridgenorth, my mother would let me buy things out of her catalogue up to the value of £1 per week. I wanted to buy a dumper truck, a bit unusual for a 13 year old but I had wanted one for so very long. Mother refused to allow me to buy one but compromised and let me buy a Landover and horse box instead, what fun I had making dirt tracks in the garden with this toy, who cared if I was 13 and supposed to be a little lady – I certainly didn't.

I do remember a few other things I did as a teenager, I used to pinch my father's clothes, things like his shirts, I loved his blazer and his trilby. I even remember trying on his underpants though that memory makes me feel very uncomfortable now.

I also can clearly recall being caught wearing some of my fathers cloth's and convincing my mother it was a fashion thing, bless her she was so gullible, I could always get away with it as long as I did my hair in a girlie style and put on a bit of make-up.

I also remember being very aware around the age of fifteen that I was sexually attracted to girls of my own age, trying even to hit on a couple of them much to their disgust.

I had been dating lads since I was about 13, however I would only let them go so far, all they seemed to want was sex. I got a bit of a reputation in that very clicky little village because I used to brag and tell real 'porkies' about how many of them had screwed me but the truth was sex was a big no no. All I really wanted was to hang around with the lads but after the magic puberty kicked in they didn't want to know me like they had before, not unless sex or something like sex was on offer. Luckily I was quite attractive and used that fully to my advantage to be around the lads, no matter what the cost.

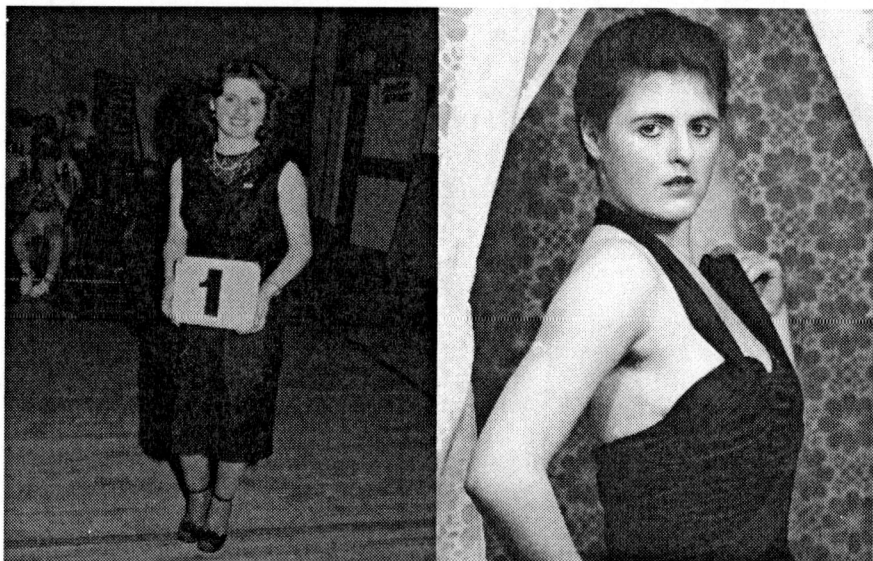

Left: 2nd place Miss Butlins' aged 14/15. Right: Modelling shot aged 18.

When I found myself being attracted to girls I do remember feeling predatory rather than giggle giggle touchy feely, feeling like I wanted them to take me seriously as a lad. Not wanting to feel like I was second class in the rutting game when I was rutting with all the other young stags, nevertheless I was seventeen before I scored my first conquest.

Lads were a push over, I could wrap them round my little finger and I had no respect for them at all. Girls were a challenge, the ultimate no no from my religions point of view, forbidden territory but so enticing. My stomach felt in my throat when we were in the changing rooms at school yet I couldn't draw the girls to me like I could the lads, a real quandary.

This first experience of being sexually active with a women was an interesting experience and not because of what I was doing to her but because of what I wouldn't let her do to me. I wanted to do everything she would let me do, touch everywhere and make her feel sexually ecstatic however when she reached for me I froze and made it quite clear that she wasn't welcome in that way.

I remember the lady in question saying how much she wanted to touch and caress me but how disgusted I felt about the prospect of allowing her that choice, much to my surprise, after waiting so long to be in that situation. After thinking long and hard about why I had reacted in such a 'keep your hands off' kind of way I have to say the root of it was whilst I was touching her I felt that predatory feeling. A desire to mount and penetrate her, feelings that were coming from deep inside my soul, feelings that were quashed when she reached for me reminding me that I was not the rutting young stag I thought I was, just a female touching another female.

It was to be another fourteen years before I found the courage to put myself in that situation again, fourteen years of denying how I felt. During those fourteen long years it feels like I lived a hundred years for other people and none for myself, putting my desires aside, throwing myself into religion, marriage, having children and being a dutiful wife and mother. All these things cost me dearly in lost opportunities and not just on a sexual level.

From sixteen to eighteen life was tough, my father had thrown me out, he just ran out of patience and I was shown the door late one night, walking the eleven miles to my boyfriend's flat in the dark and wondering what was going to become of me. I spent the next two years totally out of control, being used by one man after another, jumping from the frying pan into the fire, drinking, taking drugs, until after yet another beating from some chap and forced sex session I finally went bang and had a complete break down.

*15 nearly 16 years old, just before my father
asked me to leave the house.*

I remember one rainy afternoon, I had a small amount of money and two options, top myself to end the misery I was feeling or swallow my pride and ring my father to see if he would take me back home. I chose to ring my father and simply said 'can I come home?' To his credit he got in the car and came to get me from the side of the road. We never spoke, he understood, I believe, that I was on the edge of sanity at that point, he just got me home safely, to sanctuary, and there I remained. Spending the next three months living in my room and bathing many times a day trying to wash off all the grime I felt I had accumulated on and in my body, from two years of perversion and debauchery.

My twenties were a turbulent time with the usual kind of things people encounter in everyday life. When I pulled out of depression I went back to the religion which gave me structure and stability. I met a man and I got married at around twenty years of age, we already had one son at that point. Marriage also meant stability and although I had everything one could want around me there was nobody home in my mind. It was like I was going through the motions but not thinking about anything except pleasing everyone else; my mother, my husband, the elders of my religion, being a good parent and wife, getting god's approval, penance for what I had done in the years before.

My health was not good though, physical or mental, physically I was exhausted from having three children and several miscarriages during a nine year period. I also had cystitis from the first time I started having sex with men till the day I stopped. This led to me having kidney failure when I was 24 and mentally I was depressed, year in year out.

Yes you read correctly, I did have sex with men for many years starting at 17, I did marry, twice in fact, I did have biological children of my own. All very emotive subjects for some people who seem to see me as some sort of traitor to the cause because I tried to live as a woman before finally accepting the man within me.

Sex I felt, was not at all what it had been cracked up to be over all those years of listening to the adults around me saying everything from 'it's a duty' to 'its wonderful experience'. Sex was a necessary evil if I wanted to be a dutiful wife and children were the silver lining to the black cloud.

However this was my experience of life and I feel in some ways that it is a similar experience to male to female transwomen who often go into the Army or become body builders to prove they are real men. Sometimes it's the same for gay men in denial, who jump on any willing female they can and shag them senseless to prove they are not gay because they don't want to accept it. I think there are elements of this within my own life but not necessarily in my early twenties. I simply believe I was going through the motions and there was, as I said earlier, no one home in my mind, I had divorced myself from reality because life had been just too painful to face up to.

Sexually I was dysfunctional, a big word for in my case an inability to 'get off'. Oh I had sex all right, it's a required wifely duty to satisfy your husband and my religious up bringing, which was very male orientated, endorsed this situation. After years of putting up and shutting up I went to see my doctor who sent both myself and partner, at that time, to marriage guidance for a couple of years and then on to see a sexual therapist.

I remember that I put a lot of hope in this sex therapist, I felt so damn low in myself, I felt used by my husband. I used the term 'wanking machine' to explain exactly how I felt when engaging in sex, but after a few months of seeing the therapist I was informed that I was just one of those people who was not going to achieve orgasm and my husband had needs which I was expected to satisfy. Yes you read right, that was the advice I was given which was an endorsement of the messages I had received since childhood from the religion and because it came from someone I trusted and respected, a medical professional, I believed it and carried on living that way for many years.

During the sessions with the sex therapist I had tried to talk about how I felt about being attracted to women but not as a woman, as a man trapped inside this female shell, I told her about a fantasy that I had and on occasion, how I used to ask the male partners in my life to fulfil for me. This was around them dressing up as women, complete with make-up prior to sexual contact and that I liked to penetrate them anally with sex toys. The therapist never commented other than had I considered I was maybe lesbian? The very word lesbian I found disgusting to hear in the context of someone trying to attach it to me and my sexual orientation. I have never identified as lesbian though others have identified me in that way in their attempts to try and understand me. For people around me it has been very much a case of back to that 'sort, shift and file' that people do when trying to understand those who diversify from the socially accepted norm.

The turning point for me is clear in hindsight, the death of my father at the age of 61 in 1985.

As mentioned previously I believe my father was a tortured man, he lost himself in drink and died an early death because of it. My father had terrible experiences in World War 2 and as mentioned previously had built a museum full of military regalia which in his latter years, after taking early retirement, filled more and more of his life. Yet there was more, as mentioned earlier my father had gay tendencies, possibly being bisexual. I knew when I was younger this was the case but when he was terminally ill he spoke at length to me.

My father had in his own words been 'raped by a male orderly during the war', after the war was over he engaged from time to time in male - male sex, known by my mother but disgusting to her. It was never spoken about and when my father opened up to me shortly before his death I was left with lots of unanswered questions such as 'Why could he not accept he was Gay or Bi?' Did he have sex with men due to some scrambled feelings over being abused in the army? Was it because of his need to fit in to that socially accepted role of heterosexual male that he had not come out as gay/be? Would his life have been happier and mothers for that matter, if he had been true to his desires? There where a multitude of other questions but to cut a long and rather painful story short these opened up doors in my own mind and I found myself questioning my own motives, I did not want to live a life of regrets, I did not want to walk in the footsteps of my father.

When you have a life changing experience, such as bereavement, there is no going back from that point. For me, the passing of my father had two reactions, it left me with questions I couldn't get answers to so I turned them in on myself making me question my own life choices and secondly it infused me with energy. Losing my father felt like I had lost an arm or a leg, however the emptiness filled up with an enormous inner strength and this I believe helped me get to where I am now. I truly felt in every bone in my body that I had to understand more about who I was, I had to listen to the thoughts and feelings deep inside my soul and I had to live my life, whatever the cost, because I didn't want a life of regrets as my father had.

My father died in 1985, in 1987 my third son was born and in 1989 I filed for divorce. I did not really know where I was going with my life but I knew being married to a man was not where I wanted to be. I accepted that I was attracted to women and I also accepted that just possibly I was a man trapped in the wrong body though anyone I tried to talk to about it hadn't got a clue about where I was coming from so I kept this one to myself.

The grand plan however had a major hiccup and in 1991 I found myself once again married with a new born daughter, shortly followed by the first in a long line of transient strokes later found to be a rare form of migraine.

Now that's what you call a major hiccup don't you think?

I fought so damn hard to get away from the constraints of living my life for everybody else but made a right pig's ear of the whole thing. During my first divorce I was like a coiled spring held down by a great weight. Instead of the pressure being released slowly the weight was removed all at once and the spring took off, bounding about all over the place, with no structure or control. That's how life was for me from 1987 – 1991, life became chaotic and I made many stupid and irrational decisions.

The result of finding myself in this second marriage, exactly the same place as I had fought to get out of three years earlier, was a major and debilitating depression. I was drained of all mental energy and for a while resigned myself to the prescription drugs which dulled the pain but left my nights full of stomach cramps and sweats.

I quickly sought help from my doctor who referred me to a psychiatrist. I was convinced that I was mentally ill and the doctors at that time decide that I had non-specific bi-polar disorder. Personally I feel once again it was an undiagnosed gender issue that was the problem and fall out from having an unplanned pregnancy with resulting health complications, but doctors love labels and so that was the one they attached to me in 1992.

Two years of my life were lost to exhaustion and feeling sorry for myself, two years of taking pills that left me vegetated in the day and dreadful stomach cramps at night. One day I just woke up to what was happening around me and too me, picked myself up, dusted myself off, came off the medication. I sat my partner down telling him exactly how I felt about myself and my attraction to women, admittedly I had in fact done this when we met, yet still ended up marrying the man!

So for me the real 'history' as far as being a transman is concerned started in 1993, assisted greatly I believe by coming off female hormones, which I had been on from a teenager, almost continually. Female hormones of one kind or another, contraception pills or progesterone injections for post natal depression.

I do firmly believe that stopping female hormones was a real step forward in releasing my mind in some way. The fog I had felt in my thinking process for most of my adult life seemed to clear over a period of 12 months and clarity I had never known replaced it. Along with, interestingly enough, hair growth on my chest and face, not a lot, but dark and thick enough for me to notice and wonderfully exhilarating to me.

My attraction to women grew and grew to the point where I set about looking for sexual partners. Tentatively at first but I soon found my feet and spent the next couple of years having secret liaisons with women up and down the country answering ads in magazines and on reflection taking some damn big risks with my personal safety.

I couldn't help myself, sex was like a drug, the more I had the more I wanted. It was the only time when I felt really in touch with the male feelings inside me. The only thing I didn't like was that life was getting very complicated. I wanted to explore more about how I felt about myself, I wanted to have a relationship with a woman that wasn't just sex. I was living a dual life as a respectable married woman keeping up appearances on one side and on the other hand there was someone inside me trying desperately to break out of this shell but being forced to live a secret life.

I couldn't dress as a man, I needed to be seen by everybody as a woman, I couldn't even have a male nickname though I had a secret one from back in the 70's. It felt like I was half where I wanted to get to and half restrained because of all the people who still owned a piece of me. A particularly frustrating time in my life which dragged on forever it felt.

The change came when I met a woman in 1996 and got into a long-term relationship. At last I had a safe space to be me, or at least the part of me that I had been able to explore in restricted circumstances. Far more was waiting to break out, and that breaking out of the bonds, that transition, almost a metamorphosis began in year 2000.

Prior to 2000 I really did live a dual life. I had my daughter at home with me and my second husband, though we lived separate lives completely. I had access visits every weekend with my sons where we played 'happy families', but in the week, that was a different story.

I was part of the steering group who ran the Telford Gay Group for local lesbian, gay, bisexual and trans persons in Telford. This involved running the local entertainment evenings which were well known and well supported. This was the only place I felt I could be myself and loved every minute of it, I miss those times.

It all started with me reading an advertisement in a magazine placed there by the FTM Network. What actually caught my eye was the colour picture in the top right hand corner, a picture of a semi-naked woman looking into a full length mirror and seeing a semi naked male reflection looking back.

COMMUNITY SPIRIT

FTM London (Female To Male transgender Support Group) is one of the many many national lesbian, gay and transgender groups at this year's Community Village. Mardi Gras Guide decided to take a closer look.

"I SWAPPED MY SEX & CHANGED MY LIFE..."

Lewis is a female to male transsexual. As a fledgling 'trans-man', Lewis turned to the Female To Male transgender support group (FTM). This is his story...

"Images of transgender people are few and far between. When I was trying to come to terms with my gender identity there were few places to look for people like myself.

I transitioned in 1997 and at last could understand why I had not fitted into the lesbian world that I had tried to inhabit for 10 years.

Although it was obvious to me to identify as a gay man, other people found this harder to understand than my decision to live as a man.

Throughout my transition I continued to work and found that my employer was very supportive. A few people looked surprised when I went into the men's toilet for the first time, but we all got over that! My friends have been mostly supportive and interested in the process I have been through. Unfortunately, my family has not and I have not had any contact with them for a while.

The medical process of transition can be a difficult one, particularly in the current NHS where resources are few and far between. This usually involves hormones, chest surgery and some choose to have genital surgery, though these techniques are still far from perfect.

One of the strangest things has been going through a second adolescence with the physical and emotional changes that come with it. Spots and moods are hard to cope with when you are 34 and have to go to work, and being treated like a schoolboy in shops and on buses is not much fun.

After having always looked young for my age, and often being taken for a boy, I now find that I am gradually beginning to look a bit more my age, probably a result of the grey hairs and receding hair line.

I live a pretty ordinary life with my partner who is also a gay trans-man. This is in a way the best part of having transitioned, finally feeling that I fit with myself and with the rest of the world. I feel comfortable in my own skin at last - though like most gay men I know I would like to be taller, have a better chest and a bigger dick."

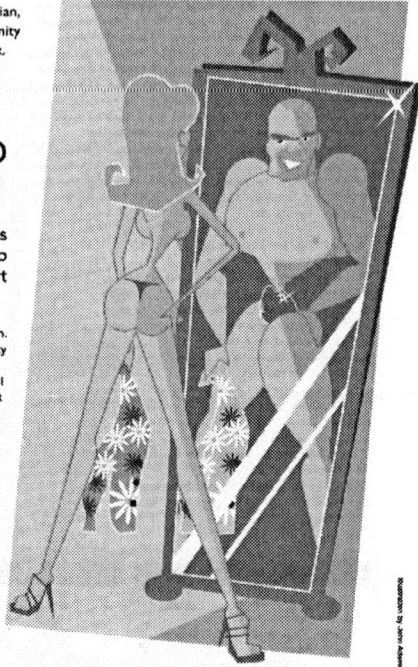

Today Lewis is an FTM committee member organising advice and support for other female to male transsexuals.

GETTING SUPPORT

FTM London. Support group for people born female who identify themselves as male. For further information, visit us in the Community Village or contact:

FTM LONDON (Female To Male Transgender Support Group): write to BM Network, London WC1N 3XX or e-mail: ftm1000@aol.com

MERMAIDS (for young trans people): Call: 07071-225895 (12 noon-9pm); BM Mermaids, London, WC1N. 3XX, e-mail mermaidsuk@geocities.com

This is the actual advert I saw which proved to be the catalyst for my own transition.

I identified with that picture so quickly and strongly that although I was in an LGBT night club with my partner at the time, everything halted. It was like time stood still and I read by the dim lights the article which explained about male to female transsexualism and how to contact the female to male network. I tore the advertisement straight out of the magazine and placed it in my pocket; the very next day I wrote to the organisation and eagerly awaited the Information Pack.

The pack arrived within a few days and along with it a copy of the 'White Book', which tells you everything you need to know about female to male transsexualism. Guess what? I was glued to the book for a couple of days, reading and re-reading. It felt amazing, I had at last got 'a name for my pain' - transsexualism, and I could do something about the way I felt, I actually had options.

My partner at that time was very hesitant, uncomfortable, and on reflection clearly threatened by my zeal to explore these options and choices I felt I had. She identified as lesbian and clearly was identifying me the same way though we had been living a male - female role in our personal lives for several years. Her own struggle to come out as lesbian was threatened by my thoughts to become more male on the outside. At that point I felt it was a real possibility that our relationship would not survive the life choices I was contemplating making for myself, to seek treatment for transsexualism.

This was a tough time for all concerned, there were no rights or wrongs, simply how it was. Once I had found out that I could change my body externally to reflect my internal identity there was no going back. I received my info pack in the June, spent two months trying to find out all I could about how to get treatment. At the same time kept a journal for myself, to detox from the enthusiasm, which I felt I could not show to those around me as they were all struggling to deal with the issue. I had my first appointment with Dr Reid, a specialist private psychiatrist in London, in the August.

My partner and I travelled together to the appointment and hardly said a word all the way there. I was anxious that the specialist would say I was not transsexual, she was anxious that he would say I was transsexual, the wait in the reception was torture.

Eventually I got into see Dr. Reid and we talked for about an hour and a half, at the end of the session he confirmed, much to my delight, that he believed I was transsexual. Because I had been trying to live as a man for two years prior to our meeting he authorized Sustanon (testosterone) injections for me to commence as soon as I was ready.

As mentioned earlier I had started a journal in the July to help me process the thoughts and feelings which had been stimulated by the information pack I had received from the FTM Network and I recorded some of my experiences about the trip to see the specialist in London. I will quote from my journal from time to time in this book though I have decided not to publish the whole journal at this time, too private.

6 Sept 00 Journal Entry

" On the 31st August I spent 14 hours travelling on 11 trains around London to find the London Institute and finally met Dr. Russell Reid....................but to cut a very long story short he felt although I had a complex history I did have a straightforward case and wrote a prescription for me there and then for Sustanon 250. I felt elated, excited, justified and redeemed, all this in one big mishmash but held it all in so as not to blow my partners mind. I know it was difficult for her.................I feel so happy and at peace over this whole issue, I really can't wait until my body starts to move through the changes"

Interestingly I wrote during this journal entry about the female hormones I had been taking for so many years, I wrote:

"You know it occurred to me only a few days ago that from 13 to 30 I was subjected to female hormones of one kind or another, raging adolescence, the pill starting with Microgynon, the ups and downs of pregnancy hormones, high doses of Progesterone to try to combat postnatal syndrome. It's no wonder I was confused mentally and physically and living a foggy existence. Only after my sterilization the effects of all those years of female hormones subsided and freed up my mind to allow, devoid of female hormonal additives, my natural development to the goal of ultimate masculinity - it would be like pumping a man full of female hormones for 14 years and wondering why he walks around In a dress, has sore boobs and is depressed out of his head – it's obvious to me if you take female hormones and you are a man you will feel like that - and that's how trapped I've felt all my life !"

I had my first injection of Sustanon 250 on 11th September 00, given to me by my very supportive Doctor. I was very excited by it and when I got back home had a photograph taken to chart the start of my transition. *See photo*

The rest is history so to speak, it's over five years since I began my transition and its been a roller coaster of a ride. However, there has never been a moment when I have regretted the decision I made or the repercussions which have occurred as a result of taking that decision. I can at last look in the mirror and see a grey haired, balding, fairly muscly, very hairy, goatee packing guy looking back with a big smile on his face - me.

One of the last times I would be seen in my previous identity, I was helping raise money for an HIV Charity as part of a dance troupe at The Planet.

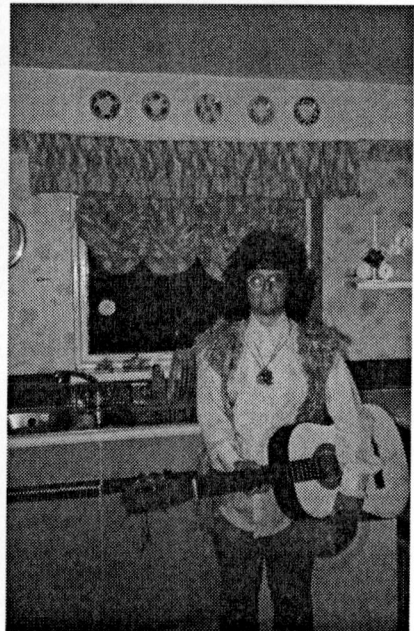

Top picture: Disney Land Paris, 2001, on holiday with my daughter

Bottom: I took every opportunity to drag it up as male prior to my transition, Colonel Custer and Ike Turner were just two examples, friends thought I was just an extrovert.

TRANSMAN

And So It Began...

BEFORE I STARTED ON A course of hormone treatment to change my body, which was something I wanted more than anything you could possible imagine, it wasn't a case of rushing in where angels fear to tread! I did do plenty of research and didn't just rely on the powers that be to tell me the facts about the side effects, pro's and con's of surgery and biological changes which could or would occur to me.

I read that the male hormones that I was requesting could in some circumstances reduce my life expectancy by up to 10 years. That the side effects included increased risk of deep vein thrombosis, heart attacks, strokes, liver problems, high blood pressure, etc. I feel it's important for you readers, to realise that I made an informed and educated choice to commence treatment for myself and would stress this as an important step for anyone considering gender reassignment.

However, keeping everything in context, I must admit that my track record for being healthy was poor and it really felt like 'I'm damned if I do and damned if I don't' over commencing treatment.

As for the possible surgical options, I also researched these for myself but to be honest I wanted to deal with one thing at a time and made my choice to initially begin male hormones. Retaining my choices as to how far I would go surgically at a later date, depending on my health, wealth and motivation.The first injection went smoothly, administered by my a nurse at the GP surgery and from that point on I had an appointment fortnightly with the local nurse for my 'shot'. I wanted very much to inject myself, my consultant had offered to teach me whilst in London although at that point the doctor's surgery were reluctant to allow me to self administer when I went on holiday and was forced to have a 'shot' early. They did finally listen to reason and allowed me to do it myself, after all, the reality was that this treatment was for life and if I had been diabetic I would have to self inject, what was the difference?

The changes started to kick in very quickly, much to my utter amazement. The first thing to change was my voice, within three injections (6 weeks) my voice broke. Admittedly it did get deeper over the next few months but there is no doubt it broke, with a nasty sore throat, after three shots. That sore throat hung around for months, every time I had a new shot it came back with a renewed vigour and it felt like it would never go. I had no infection in the throat, just a very painful voice box.

Once my voice had broken I lost the ability to sing which was a sadness for me, I had my voice trained in 1985 and enjoyed singing immensely. However, I knew this would be a possibility and it came with the turf. I just felt just sad to be no longer able to express my emotions through song.

I do still try and sing, much to the annoyance of friends and family, and have often thought about having my voice retrained or at least going to see a speech therapist to see if this is a possibility, maybe one day.

Body hair growth also developed quickly but it was deceptive. Initially I was devastated because as already mentioned I did have some chest hairs which started to grow after I stopped taking female hormones in 1991 and they fell out very quickly after I started my shots! I thought for a few awful weeks that I was going to be one of those smooth, sleek types and I wanted to be a bear! However, after breaking out in masses of small red pimples each spot proceeded to grow a hair, I had my wish, a bear was born.

My sex drive was one of the real big changes, I had been warned that the Sustanon affected your sex drive for the better. Something I had never really had but I felt like a prowling lion all the time. It gave me a real insight into how my adolescent sons must have felt after all that's what I was going through, adolescence at the grand old age of 37.

Left: The earliest photo, at about the 6 months point.
Right: Even wearing a binder I struggled to hide my breasts.

The body fats redistributed over a period of 6 months or so to give me more of a male physique and where I had almost no muscle tone to begin with, the hormones along with a lot of body building gave me a reasonable muscle development. Though I soon realized there is a limit to what the hormones could do to a small framed person like myself. I was never going to be 'Adonis'.

The next amazing, almost unbelievable, change which hit like a two edge sword was the changes to my clitoris. It grew into a small penis, complete with foreskin, which retracted over the head like any other guy and complete with erections.

The growth was at times very uncomfortable, I felt stretched and engorged most of the time but the unexpected blow was that as my penis grew I started to lose sensitivity. It felt like I had more size and could achieve erections but the nerves did not seem to keep up, the result was it got harder to achieve the big O.

About 11 months into taking the hormone I wrote a review in my journal as follows:

14.08.01 - Review

"Since I took my first shot of Sustanon many things have changed first and foremost my personal appearance and development.

I have developed a good all over growth of body hair and support a goatee, moustache and sideburns with a slight receding of the hair line. My voice is as deep as I think it can get, body muscle is developing slowly. I pass now 100% of the time except where someone knew me before, with them a mixed bag of reactions can clearly be observed.

DR Reid and my own inner thoughts were right......................... my relationship failed with my ex-partner, she moved out in July.

Everything seems to be churning and clicking around in my life as the cogs of chaos re-align for the next decade of my life. Funny, looking back it seems towards the end of my teens, twenties, and now thirties, a major upheaval occurred and life is reborn into something different and amazing. Stretching my horizons even further in the growth of my inner being.

I feel sad for the loss of my relationship but hopeful and optimistic for future developments. I feel strongly that there is someone waiting for me to come into their life...................PS: sexual relief is a daily necessity, never thought it would ever be like this"

Apart from the physical changes which occurred, my mind started to change. My thinking processes, my drives, my masculinity (which I had always felt was present) became clearer and as a person I became calmer, more focused, more balanced.

I remember a conversation with a volunteer staffing the out of hours support line for the FTM Network who said 'If you think you feel 'male' now wait till you start the hormones' and to be honest I couldn't see how I would 'feel' more male but he was right, I did. This has been mentioned to me by others and they describe it as a breadth and depth to the feelings of being male, I feel that's a fair description.

For instance during sex, the desire to penetrate began to couple with the need to ejaculate, this then grew into a feeling that I had ejaculated, even though this was physically impossible, totally illogical, but nevertheless a fact.

I recorded many thoughts in my diary around this period of development but most of them are triple x rated so best not include them all. One quote which will give you an insight into how my mind was working went as follows:

6.3.02

"My emotions have totally settled, I have none of the extremes which plagued the bulk of my life and in most things this is good but whether its good for sex is a different kettle of fish. I do feel passion when I get sexually aroused, strong desires to be inside my partner and waves of strong emotions hitting me but is this lust or love because once sex is over so are the emotions, or could it be the male drive to 'mate' is all consuming and when the task is complete you are at peace within yourself

It became very frustrating that my innerself was evolving faster than my body, some would say that it was because I was dressing as a male, striving to be treated as a male and acknowledged by a few people as actually being male. Was this why I felt more male? Whether this is true or not I cannot say, I only know what I felt. I did feel that every day in every way I was escaping the confines of my outer shell and the man inside was finally standing upright, standing tall, even though I was only 4ft 11 inches at that point.

Now that's another interesting fact, I was clearly told that the hormones would not make me grow in stature but I did grow. I gained two inches in height and went up a shoe size, a very welcome but unexpected side effect of my transition.

During the rest of this book I will break down other developments and experiences of my transition into short sections. I will look at sex, surgery, family and where I am now in my life. I feel it will be easier for you the reader, to follow the changes if I explain them in this way, bit size chunks so to speak and we will look firstly at, getting rid of our unwanted, for a guy, breasts.

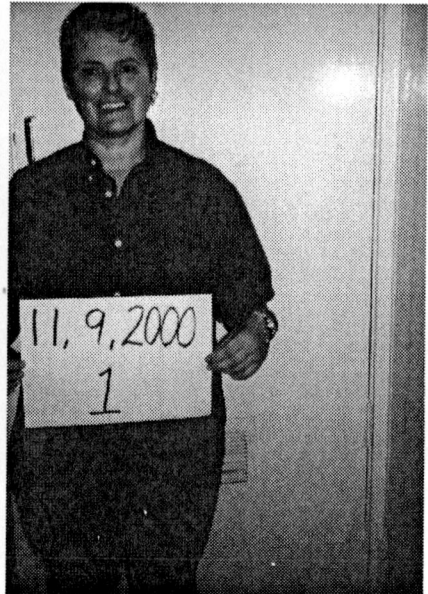

*Left: A photo of me in 1999 when I was trying to live
in society, to the best of my ability, as a man.*

Right: The photo of my first injection, see the beaming smile!

TRANSMAN

Breast Is Not Always Best

ONE OF THE FIRST PROBLEMS facing a transitioning female to male is the visible presence of boobs. You don't want to see them, feel them yourself, want anyone else to feel them, the very external symbol of being a woman, when you are a guy, is unbearable.

If you are small chested you can perhaps wear a baggy shirt and get away with hiding them without too much trouble but if you are a little on the larger side baggy shirts don't work and you come up with many varied ways of hiding them away.

I tried all the usual sports gear to flatten off their protuberance from under my shirt, but to no avail, and in the end purchased some tubular elasticated bandage and made for myself a very very tight binder. There are various specially produced under garments that can be purchased, usually over the net and from America, but for me, as money was tight and motivation high, I experimented until I found something that worked.

This binding however was like a drug and it got to the point where I was wearing the binder 24 hours a day. I started to get muscle wastage and backache but at that time I would rather suffer those side effects of wearing the binder than to have to look at and acknowledge breasts. Being flat chested looked and felt so damn good, it was addictive and I just couldn't break the habit even when it started to make me suffer physically.

Feelings like these, the need to remove the most visible female give away when you're trying to live as a male, lead to the one op that most trans guys want done yesterday. The bilateral subcutaneous mastectomy, a big term for what is simply the removal of the breasts and the construction of a male appearance chest.

I was clearly warned by my psychiatrist to be patient and not to go to a local surgeon, but did not listen. I inquired about having the op done privately but at a bill of two thousand pounds I was priced out of the market. My ex offered to pay for the surgery but my controlling nature wouldn't let me accept her offer, by controlling I mean wanting to be fully in charge of my transition and not reliant or indebted to anyone. No, reason went out of the window and when offered an appointment to see a local surgeon wild horses couldn't have kept me away.

After having the initial meeting with a local surgeon, which went well, he had convinced me that as a surgeon he was experienced in the procedure I was requesting. They had apparently operated on guys like myself before, I felt confident and agreed to proceed with the surgery. The wait was only a matter of three/four months but it felt like a life time

The appointment came through for September 2001 and although I went in with realistic expectations I did of course have high hopes that my chest surgery would leave me in a liveable state of body. A state where I could at least wear a shirt next to my skin without the need for a binder anymore.

I recorded much in my journal over this period of time but will just explore some quotes as follows:

25 09 01 - waiting for a bed
"This morning was one of the most unbelievably stressful experiences of my entire life. I waited for a bed for five hours with a lead weight in my stomach, sweat pouring out of my whole body and anger and frustration burning in my heart. I have for the weeks and days leading up to today been so calm and collected, I was totally unprepared for such overwhelming feelings of being distraught at the possibility of postponement!

29 09 01
Yesterday the surgeon came to see me and gave me some bad news, the internal stitches had given way and the nipples had dropped, I would need further surgery in three months or so.

25 11 01

It has now been 6 weeks since my surgery and my chest looks bloody dreadful, I have two disfigured hanging sacks of different sizes on my chest and am fighting infections in both nipples every day. I feel at the moment that at my next appointment with the surgeon I will ask them for a complete mastectomy, nipples and all, my chest is hideous and I can't stand to look at it ".

The surgical technique used on me was inappropriate for the size of my breasts. Though the procedure may have been successful for small breasted females it was clearly not the option for myself and should not have been attempted. However, I did return to see the surgeon requesting a total mastectomy saying that I would have tattoo's for nipples at a later date. After listening to them say that the results could be improved, they could make this better, I agreed to have a second operation.

6.3.02

"It is now five days since I had my second chest op and the results are poor, the right side is slightly better than the left. The left is very poor with deep vertical crevices, deep enough for you to put your fingers into sitting, either side of the nipple, the one nipple has the appearance of a figure 8....................., I will be patient, perhaps the appearance will improve with time but my gut tells me it won't".

23 05 02 - next consultation with psychiatrist

"Last week I had my next meeting in London........firstly he looked at my chest and was clearly appalled by how it looked, saying 'in all his time of working with transmen he had only seen one case worse and that surgeon had been struck off. The doctor asked me if he could write as a matter of urgency to a plastic surgeon, on my behalf, to request an early appointment to review my situation, I agreed"

To cut a very long story short, my chest was a mess. As I said previously the surgical procedure attempted on myself was wholly inappropriate.

Clearly I have to accept some blame for this myself. I was impatient like a lot of guys in my situation, but a do feel the surgeon should have thought long and hard about operating on me in the first place. I did take action in trying to stop the surgeon in question from using this procedure on other men who came after me but to no avail. I did manage to get an admission that in my case an error of judgment had been made but it was felt the procedure was appropriate. If I remember correctly they stated 'just because a procedure is not effective on one patient is not a reason to stop performing that procedure on others'. I feel personally that if one person is mutilated by a procedure then why take the risk with someone else? Only my opinion but a valid one I believe.

I did get to see a plastic surgeon, Mr. Davies at Charring Cross Hospital and I quote:

08 08 02

"Mr. Davies said to me that too much skin had been taken from the wrong places which left him with not enough tissue to work with to put this right, he could remove all the cut and scarred tissue away but I would be left with two lateral incisions across my chest much higher than where they should be. He would try and save the nipples by removing them, reshaping them and grafting them on to where they should be"

This is what he did. I went in for surgery in October 03 and am very pleased with the result all things considered.

I wrote in my journal some thoughts prior to the last operation I had on my chest:

28.10.03

"So, here we go again, this will be the last time I let them oper-ate on my chest this much, I have firmly decided.

Well, I'm sitting here in Charring Cross hospital. I had to pick myself up by the scruff of the neck and drag myself to the hospital but I'm here and committed to going through the op once more.

I feel peaceful, a little alone, though I am in a room on my own so I would be feeling alone, I am settled in myself and just waiting for tomorrow............

02.11.03
(After the op)
The op is all over and I am back home, early results are promising but the cut, armpit to armpit except an inch in the middle is drastic. I believe the team did the best they could and am not complaining, my chest is flat and tight. The nipples have been made a lot smaller than they would have been but this was at my request, it is too early to know if the grafts will take but I am hopeful"

The hospital notes stated that they had redone a bilateral subcutaneous mastectomy, its not perfect but liveable. I can now at least wear a shirt without a T-shirt or thick vest underneath and I can look in the mirror and admire the view. Next time I go on holiday I will be able to take my shirt of on the beach and amaze people with my stories of surviving an attack by a killer shark which left me with a cut from armpit to armpit. Role on the next 'you show me yours and I will show you mine' testosterone fuelled scar competition over a pint, mine will take some beating I can tell you!

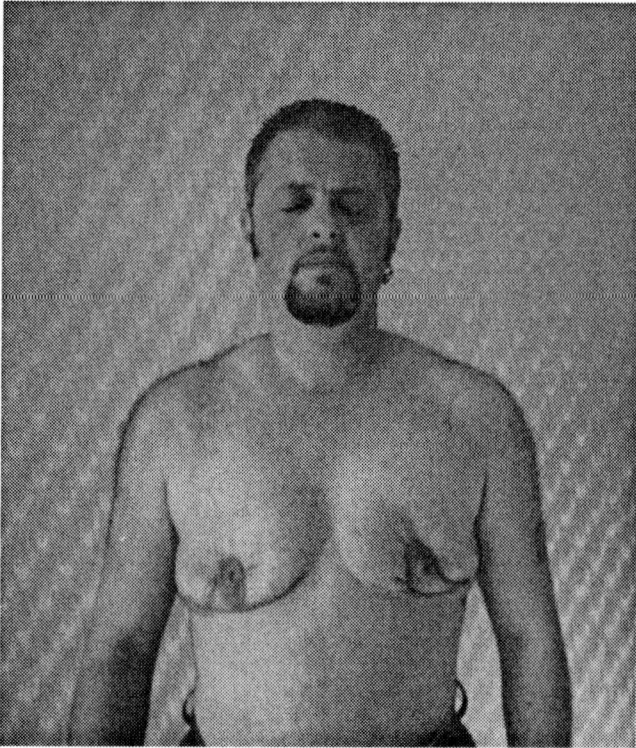

After the first operation, September 2001

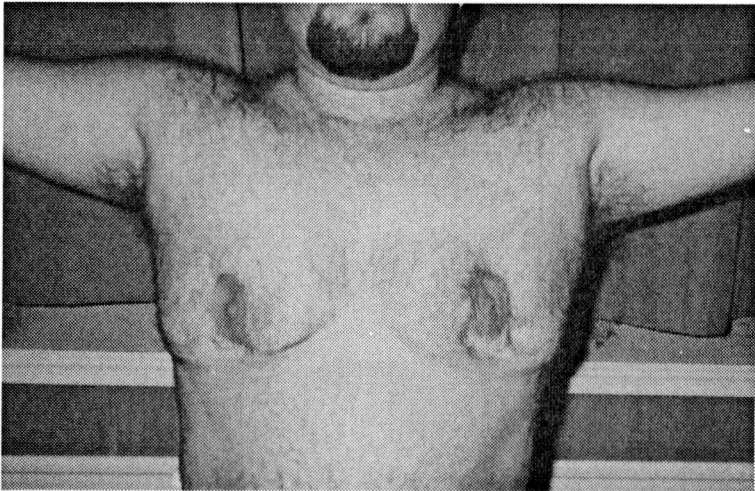

After 2nd operation in March 2002 and prior to final op.

TRANSMAN

Sex Stuff

THE DEFINITIONS OF THE WORD 'sexuality' as I understand them to be are complex to say the least and this is coming from a person who teaches the basics of Human Sexuality as a job. I work as a trainer not only teaching the basics on the above subject, but also 'Safer Sex' and 'HIV prevention' and most importantly of all 'Trans Awareness Training'. However, when it comes to my own sexuality I process my thoughts and feelings relentlessly and struggle to grasp an understanding of my own mechanisms both physical and psychological.

Firstly you have to look at sexuality as a subject and decide what it means to you. Does it mean your gender, does it mean your sexual orientation, does it represent the sexual picture of 'who you are' that we present to the world or does it encompass the sexual being that resides within your shell of a body, or is it all of these at some time or other in your life?

Some say Gender Identity is in the mind and sex is between the legs, others would describe it very differently. Painter and Adams put together one of the best templates I've seen for explaining sexuality as being a 'gestalt', the whole of an individual, looking at emotional needs, sexual experiences, spiritual needs, political affiliations and more. I believe this template is very inclusive of all walks of life and gender identities and encapsulates all facets of that person under the title of sexuality.

For me that isn't quite it, sexuality transfers in my mind to the biological sexual act, positive or negative, functional or dysfunctional, possible or impossible, the needs and drives which haunt my need for intimate sexual experiences.

Being a sexually active person who has the complexity of being trans-sexual can take me to the heights of ecstasy and to the depths of despair all in one sexual encounter. Consistency is hard to achieve yet the drive to have sexual contact with another person is something that is ever present, heightened by injecting necessary Sustanon and fed by the hunger of a psychological need to penetrate.

The mechanics of being sexually active are far from simple for guys like me because we lack the biological organs on our body but the drive to use that organ is in our minds. How can the mind and body find a happy medium when no penis is present? A question I live with and an answer I search for every time I make love and things don't quite go the way they should.

I have spoken with transmen who say they do not need a sexual aid in their sex act, mimicking the movements of penetrating is all they need to achieve climax but this is not the answer for me. Others still have the desire to be penetrated themselves using what nature has given them for sexual pleasure and feeling no adverse reaction to engaging in being penetrated; once again this is not for me. Still others get their rocks off by rubbing their micro penis between the buttocks of their sexual partner for maximum friction and they get what they need from that experience but not me. No my needs are very specific and I struggle to find a happy medium as others have so am left with the original question; 'How can the mind and body find a happy medium when no penis is present?'

Along with this question I repeatedly ask myself in a search for sexual peace go the fears and insecurities which live just under the surface of my innerself. The fear is not all consuming and the insecurities do not fill up my mind constantly, yet are present and to ignore them is to deny the reality of what being in a heterosexual relationship means to me. The man I am wants to satisfy the woman I love and share intimate moments with. The fears manifest themselves in thoughts such as 'will she tell the difference', 'will she miss something that she had or felt with a biological male', fears of inadequacy which can be crippling if you allow them to take hold. However, putting them in context, fears which most men have at one time or another in their life, good old fashioned 'performance anxiety', no more no less.

I openly acknowledge and embrace these thoughts but keep a balanced perspective. A partner who engages in a sexual act with me makes a choice to do so, well aware of my trans status, and I give all that I have to that love making session. I empower myself by turning a negative into a positive in my mind, the positive being these fears which all men feel at some time in their lives are yet reinforcing I am no different to other men, and in the arms of my lover I spread my wings and fly.

I recorded in my journal some quite deep thoughts over my biological situation versus my inner drives:

22.12.00

"It occurs to me that being FTM and trying to understand the needs and desires of both my mind and body, that in my effort to accept my need to be male, I need to accept that my biology is female in anatomy and thus achieve sexual satisfaction with my growing clitoris which I obviously identify as my penis.

I have to painfully accept and understand, learn techniques of stimulating my clitoris rather than expect that I can achieve satisfaction using my clitoris as a penis. This, in direct contradiction to the needs of my mind, which beyond any shadow of a doubt sees my growing penis as a physical presence representing my penal shaft. I have had to shut off that it is a female organ and therein lies the root of my sexual dysfunction, my body is female, anatomically female so I must find a satisfactory union between my minds needs and my body's need to achieve sexual relief.

An example of this is referred to by Masters & Johnson as the plateau phase of clitoral stimulation. My mental and physical desire is as I move towards orgasm, that my penis should become longer and harder so that I can penetrate my partner. Though this is impossible for me to do but is in direct opposition to what M & J say, they state that in preparation for orgasm the female clitoris retracts beneath the foreskin and this raises questions for the FTM.

For instance: Do the hormones develop the clitoris and hood so that it stands erect and no longer retracts at the plateau phase? (When you're just about to blow). If this is the case, then some kind of penetration maybe possible with the fully developed micro-penis.

Does the growth of this organ, aided by the Sustanon, mean that the normal physiological functions of the clitoris break down and the reaction of the new 'penile' tissue, following the pattern of male erection (get bigger instead of retract,) become the norm. Is this part of the learning curve one must experience as part of becoming male in body?

Is it in fact possible to treat your growing clit as a penis or to do this means you sacrifice the ability to get off?

Well, some deep thinking there and I have only used an excerpt from my journal. What actually fuelled these thoughts was, as I said previously, as my body grew my sensitivity got less, my body reacted differently to the sexual experience and I got stuck at the plateau phase every time, this was a painful time. I had to accept certain biological limitations to my transition and only by embracing these limitations did I free my mind to become functional again.

What is interesting, is the above quote from my diary was written before my genital area had fully developed from the use of male hormones. The process as described by Masters & Johnson, of female orgasms with the clitoris retracting, did in fact change totally to fall more in line with the male pattern of sexual development, the micro-penis does became erect and larger immediately prior to orgasm and then spasms as if releasing sperm during the climax phase, fascinating to experience.

There are surgical options for those who cannot find a workable solution to the lack of inches needed to penetrate and satisfy the sexual hunger which plagues some of us but I wonder if surgery is the answer for all transmen.

The genital reconstruction surgery which is available has two main options that of phalloplasty and metiodioplasty. Both are risky, both involve building a scrotum with testicular implants, both include extending the urethra so that you can vent standing up and both give you an appearance of a penis. Setting the risk elements aside both are viable options however the sexual functioning ability is different in the two surgical options, and I feel one must educate yourself fully before choosing either option.

The more invasive of the two techniques, phalloplasty, involves using tissue, a considerable amount of tissue, from either the abdomen or arm and although I am not a medical professional I certainly have enough knowledge from talking to guys who have had surgery or gleaned from medical documents and photographs to see that this complex process is fraught with possible complications. The final stage of this technique being the insertion of a device to allow erections to be simulated is an interesting option but the device has a life of only ten years, then the surgery starts again.

Even though a transman may choose to put himself through this surgical procedure there are limitations to how valuable it will be to him and as we are talking about 'sex stuff' lets stick with that thought. It will not be his micropenis (formally his clitoris) penetrating his sexual partner so stimulating the phallus will not itself achieve orgasm. If the forearm is used for the surgery there will be sensitivity, the knowledge that a part of his body is penetrating his partner with everything fitting into about the right place as it should but he will still not be able ejaculate. He will not be able to jerk off as and when the need arises, as other men do, this will still require his stimulating the micro penis. I could go on but I think I've made my point.

The other procedure, metiodioplasty, is I feel a more realistic option and one I may consider at a future date for myself. This uses the development which has occurred with the assistance of Sustanon, the micro penis, and releases those tissues which have grown inside the body held back by the restrictions of the hood of the micropenis, releasing them to come out of the body. The appearance is a more natural and realistic look, orgasms are achieved by stimulating this micropenis, penetration is probably still not possible depending on how flexible you and your partner are in the positions of the Karma Sutra but erections will be clearly evident and no big scar will be visible on the arm or abdomen. With this procedure and phalloplasty it is still possible for the urethra to be rerouted to allow venting whilst standing at a urinal if, in the case of metiodioplasty, enough tissue has been released to pass through the fly of your trousers.

For my part I have made a choice to not have phalloplasty. I have taken three years out to make a decision over metiodoplasty and I feel still stuck on the fence over whether to proceed or not. I made a choice in May 04 to put myself on national television so that the voice of men who choose not to have this surgery could be heard as the other guest speaker had in fact chosen to and followed through with phalloplasty. I felt it important that men who do not have this surgery are not seen any the less as men. To not have this surgery is a hard choice to make when everything that makes you feel male makes you feel to some extent inadequate without the penis being present. However, it is possible to find that middle road between changing your body to be as male as it can be, having essential surgery and then learning to live with the micro-penis as opposed to a surgically created penis. This will always be a personal and emotive discussion between men of transsexual origins and I respect both sides of the argument.

For myself I have learnt to use prosthetics to do all those tasks which my body is unable to do due to my biological differences from being a natural born male. These were not the easiest of lessons to learn but serve me well, I adapted, almost as a person with a disability would adapt to not having a limb.

Some of the drawbacks of not having surgery, in real terms, are those times when you come under public scrutiny, in the changing rooms of the gym, swimming or bathing on the beach, medical examinations or, god forbid, in the accident and emergency room if something should happen to you.

The big one of course is when you find yourself sexually attracted to a prospective new partner, how do you tell them you don't have a penis as they understand one to be. You can joke about it, after all having sex with someone like myself is very low risk of catching STIs, no need for contraception as there is no risk of pregnancy, no risk of not being a big enough boy, you can negotiate your own size and no risk of losing the erection just because the guys got off. He can keep it going all night if she wants it - but she won't get flesh and blood, she won't feel his warmth inside her, it will be cold.

There lies another quandary, if you have had surgery and the results are realistic (big if), do you tell your partner you were born female or do you keep the secret and hope nobody ever finds out. Sexually if she/he looks close enough they will tell the difference although love is blind they say and you may be able to 'blag' it. A debate which will become more evident now the gender recognition act has become law and we are able to get married like other men do.

Love makes it real, if two people love each other they don't notice the differences or if they do it doesn't seem to matter. That's my experience anyway, I can't speak for anyone else. I would however be lying if I said I didn't long to feel real connection with my lover, the way it should be naturally between a man and woman. As humans our imagination is a wonderful blessing and fills in the gaps that nature has left in our bodies and after all the largest sex organ in our bodies is the brain, get it straight in your mind and the body follows.

TRANSMAN

Out Of Sight - Out Of Mind?

From the first time I started talking to other transmen about their operations it became very clear to me that many of them did not intend to have a hysterectomy.

The first time I rang the FTM Networks' Wednesday evening support line I spoke to a guy who talked about his life as a transman and naturally I asked him about what operations he had had and his experiences of transition. This guy had only had a chest op and had no intention of having further surgery including a hysterectomy. I remember asking him why not and he replying 'The hormones stop my periods, I can't see it so as far as I am concerned its not there and I can't see why I need to put myself through that surgery and I'm not alone, most guys don't have a hysterectomy'.

This seemed to make sense at the time and I didn't question him further but decided to keep an open mind for myself and research the pro's and con's of surgery when the time was right.

Well, the guy had been right, very quickly the Sustanon stopped any menstruation and it was very much a case of out of sight out of mind. However, I did wonder from time to time about the long term effects of high doses of testosterone on the womb and ovaries, it couldn't be good for you and so decided to raise the subject with my Consultant and GP.

The Consultant Psychiatrist was very clear, a hysterectomy was recommended at around the two year point of taking Sustanon. Of course the choice was mine as to whether I proceeded or not but if I chose not to, then I ran the risk of developing 'break-through bleeding' a much higher risk of 'ovarian cancer'. I would require regular smear tests and would have to stay on high doses of Sustanon to combat the production of female hormones from the ovaries for years and years with this bringing health risks of its own.

I felt like I had a time bomb ticking away inside me that could go bang at any time in my future. My male future, the one I had fought hard to take from fantasy to reality and the future I didn't want being haunted by gynaecological problems. I knew that for me I could not sit and wait for something to happen which would require emergency treatment. No, I would have to face the fear and push for surgery and so this is what I did.

After talking with my Consultant in London he wrote to a phalloplasty surgeon to see if I would need a special kind of hysterectomy due to my prior gynaecological history, four caesareans, several miscarriages and sterilization. The answer came back from the surgeon that if I was planning on having phalloplasty the hysterectomy could be done at the same time if not then a local surgeon was perfectly capable of doing the operation for me.

At that time I was not contemplating phalloplasty, I wanted to deal with one thing at a time and so my doctor referred me through to a local gynaecologist who was happy to see me. The appointment was set for November 02, around my fortieth birthday.

The thought of having this surgery was very distressing to me. Back in 1991 I had reached a point where I couldn't tolerate anyone, medical or personally, messing with me in that area of my body. I had refused point blank to have anymore smears or swabs, it was simply a no-go area on my body. I hated the thought of having to be examined, operated on, catheterized, stitched, packed, or whatever was involved with a hysterectomy, my mind was in turmoil over the whole subject of going for this surgery. Never the less, logic told me this had to be done and I went into the first appointment with the surgeon with much apprehension, distrust, and emotional upheaval wondering how the hell I was going to survive this life choice without having a heart attack from the stress !

I recorded many thoughts and feelings in my journal around this period in my life; I will quote firstly from that initial appointment:

21.11.02

*"Last Friday I met with the gynaecologist and we spoke openly about the pro's and con's of having a hysterectomy. She said clearly that they could only remove the womb, ovaries and cervix, in this country they do not remove the vaginal cavity, She was very frank with me stating that my insides would be full of scar tissue from previous operations, that she would have to go a fifth time into my old caesarean scar. She said that my bladder could be a problem because of scar tissue and there could be holes in it and in a worst case scenario I may come out of hospital with the catheter still in place to allow the bladder to heal. The doctor told me that the op would be very much like having another caesarean section but worse and this time the catheter would be in place for several days while I healed................... I requested a month to consider what she had said to me and make my decision as to whether I was going to proceed or not. She agreed that this was OK, we made an appointment for the 13th December to meet again..........................
I know the operation is necessary, at the moment I am fit and well so it seems the time to get it done"*

The appointment had gone pretty much as I had expected it to. I knew my insides would be a problem and after years of bladder problems I had already figured there may be difficulties, but I took the month to think about my choice after all it was my choice. Other guys did not have the surgery and if I didn't want to or wasn't ready yet then I would make the choice not to proceed, a difficult and long month but I did return to meet with the surgeon on the 13th December

19.12.02

On Friday I had my second appointment with the surgeon and I told her that I had made my decision, I had decided to proceed with the surgery. She once again stated that it could be a heavy operation with complications to the bowel and bladder depending upon the level of scar tissue which could not be assessed until I had been opened up. I signed a form to say I accepted this was the case and now it's just sit and wait, AGAIN"

I could write a whole book on the next twelve weeks, that how long it took for the operation to come round. However the real story was in how it felt to wait, those twelve weeks felt like twelve years and I found myself doing some very out of character and practical things to prepare for this surgery. I had a real sense of foreboding and even felt the need to write my will, of all things, to make my peace with a few old skeletons in the cupboard and clarify my position with my life insurance - heavy stuff.

You know the real freaky thing which nobody on this earth could have planned, was I went down to theatre for my operation to remove my womb and ovaries at the same date and time (only 21 years later), that I was first opened up by caesarean, in that same wound and the same hospital, for the birth of my first child.

I had gone full circle, from the ultimate act of a female, giving life from your womb to your child, to the ultimate act of a transman, the removal of your womb, that which signifies womanhood, from your body. It felt like rebirth, it felt like healing from all those years of hating my body, it empowered me as the shackles of 'female' were removed from my person for good.

After all the worrying the operation went well and the surgeon came to see me a few days later to tell me how it had gone from her point of view. Apparently I had both forms of endometriosis and the tissue of the uterus was crispy, in her own words she said 'I had the uterus of a ninety year old female'. She said it would not have lasted much longer without it causing me some big problems. I had only been on the Sustanon for two years or so, there are guys out there who have been on hormones for many years and still haven't had their hysterectomy, imagine the state their insides may be in.

The hospital staff allowed me to keep my dignity and placed me in a male ward, I removed my own catheter from my bladder and on returning home I removed my own stitches though I would not recommend this for the faint of heart. Anything I could do for myself they allowed me to do, thus retaining some control over my own treatment and choices.

I wrote to the hospital after I had been discharged and thanked them for what they had done for me, how they had allowed me to retain my dignity in all areas of how they treated me. I have since recommended the same gynaecological team to other guys in this area and out of this area.

One final thought on this subject is the positive effects of making the choice to have my operation and there have been some unexpected ones.

Once the ovaries had been removed I had a flush of new hair growth, muscle growth and penis development, my sexual experiences were heightened by a marked increase in strength of erection and orgasms.

The big one of course is I now don't have any worries for my future, no ghosts from the 'fem' past waiting to creep up on me. I am free, I am empowered and I am happy.

TRANSMAN

You Can't Choose Your Family...

THERE ARE NOT MANY PEOPLE who can say they have been in one lifetime, Mother and Father, Daughter and Son, Wife and Husband, Aunt and Uncle, Sister and Brother, and thankfully only Grandfather. So to ask how my family dealt with my transition is not an easy question to answer, to say the least.

Families are complex, as are any human relationships. To add in trans issues to a family unit, issues around how to accept, understand or even just interact with a trans person is challenging. To watch a daughter or sister, who has all societies' trappings of living in that female gender role change to a son or brother, with very different gender role expectations, makes the task very challenging for all concerned.

There are families who disown the trans person, some are supportive to a point, others try to find out all they can on the subject of transsexualism. They try to educate themselves on how best to adapt to this new family situation, while the remainder don't see the change as anything of any significance and continue to see the person inside the outer shell and relate to them just as they did before.

I decided when it came to talking to my family members that I would try and keep them as included as possible in the process, to a point anyway. There where certain things I did not tell them and the motive for this was purely to protect them from how they might feel if certain facts where made known. For instance, my diagnostic letter talks about my parents, information I thought was given in a confidential environment was reproduced in this important document. I felt it inappropriate to show this paperwork to my surviving parent who would only have been saddened by what she read.

I had not only a parent to consider but a brother, sister, and four biological children, each of these people needed to be talked to in different ways. Setting aside my extended family of nephews, nieces, cousins, uncles and aunts and anyone else who would come out of the closet once this juicy bit of gossip got out.

I don't really remember who I told first but I think it was my mother. I tried to keep it simple out of respect for her age and so just explained that I had always felt that I should have been born a male. I helped her recall conversations I had had with her throughout my adult life reflecting elements of the longing to have a male identity in society. I told her before I went to London to see the specialist and she was another who hoped my diagnosis would be that I was not trans.

Most mothers, indeed parents reactions are predictable, they feel that it was all their fault, a mother feels that she must have done something wrong when she was pregnant. Sometimes parents feel very strongly that you are not trans at all, to the point where they feel a great medical blunder is being made in treating you for transsexualism. At one time my own mother intended to travel to London to see my Consultant to give him a piece of her mind. Clearly parents go through a grieving processing of losing a daughter and have to work on the gaining a son bit, only time and patience will deal with this one. Recently my Mother has said to me that because of the new Gender Recognition Act and the fact that I will shortly be able to get my new birth certificate reflecting my birth gender as male, at that point she will accept that she has a son and not a daughter, time will tell.

On the eve of my first operation my mother rang the hospital to try and talk me out of surgery:

> *25.09.01*
> *"......mother rang me last night trying to put doubts into my mind about the op, which I expected but was very uncomfortable with. My answer was short and simple "if I didn't want the operation mother then I wouldn't be here in the first place", I felt so*

damn angry that she couldn't at least wish me luck but chose not to say anything, wasn't worth the agro........"

This was particularly difficult for me to deal with in that I felt very alone waiting for my operation. No partner, no family support and not many that I would call 'friend' to look to for support and one would expect support when a parent rings at the eleventh hour not pressure tactics to talk you out of your choices. As a parent myself I understood her fears however I had to point out repeatedly that I was a mature adult making educated and informed choices for myself, choices she may not agree with but nevertheless had to accept were my choices and not hers.

The grape vine in my family is an extraordinarily efficient machine and knowing this I felt it was important to speak to other family members sooner rather than later.

Telling ones siblings, brothers and sisters is just as difficult and complex as telling your parents. I have a brother and a sister, both are much older than I and both have struggled with coming to terms with my transition.

Just the knowledge of me writing this book has stirred up a cascade of emotions within my family. As if they feel that by me having a book printed there will be no going back for me or them, almost like up until now there was an opt out clause for us all and once something is in print that choice has gone for ever.

I feel it in inappropriate to discuss at length my brother and sister but will say a few things about the situation.

Firstly both of them have supported me to the best of their ability and will continue to do so. Our family are not close or affectionate but when the going gets tough we do stick together and as a family unit we have had far more challenging issues to deal with than a transsexual in the family, I can assure you.

There has never been the kind of statement, 'if you transition we will never speak to you again' although I was told that it would have been best if I had moved away and transitioned somewhere else.

I think that the thought behind this was to hang onto memories of who I was and they would not have had to face the visual image of me becoming someone else. Someone they really did not want to get to know even though, as I said previously, I believe they have done their best to support me.

Telling my children, even my adult children, was the hardest thing for me to do. As indeed it would be for any parent trying to find the right words to say you are still going to be their mother but not have any of the characteristics which they would expect from a mother. In fact you're going to be more like society's perceptions of a father but at the same time you don't want to take the place of their father - a non entity parent who nevertheless still loves them and intends to stay in their lives if they would have you.

I remember searching on the net trying to talk to other guys with kids to find out how they had managed, but with not much luck, in the end I decided to go with my gut feeling and told them how I felt.

My biological children, Xmas 2004, who are a constant source of inspiration to me.

If I'm totally honest I had to some extent drip fed them for years by saying things like, 'I felt I should have been a boy' and 'if I could choose I would be a boy like you' to my sons. Because I had raised the issue before it was easier to build on those conversations, this time the conversation was more focused and I had to make it clear to them not only did I feel like I should have been a boy but that I was intending to do something about how I felt and would probably change my body to look like a boy.

Luckily I was able to tell three of my four children to their faces about my plan of action, the fourth was more difficult, a couple of years prior to my decision to transition my one son had cut off contact for various reasons revolving around being thirteen years of age and having raging emotions and needs to simplify his life. This put me in the difficult position of having to tell him by post, not ideal at all as there was no opportunity to answer questions he may have had, but he had the right to know like the others and the right to know from me, not someone else.

I made mistakes, in hindsight I know I did, I feel I could have handled telling my children better, in particular with my youngest and probably the others too. However, there were no books to read, no one to talk to about the rights and wrongs of helping children through my transition process. What to tell them and when, how to interact with them in my new gender role, how they should interact with you in your new parental role, how to deal with schools, their other parent, their sense of loss. The list is endless and only by going through the experience of it all can you gain an insight, now at least I can help other family men in my situation.

Hand on heart I know I did the best I could and thankfully all my children are in contact with me. The youngest has recently gone to live with her biological father, a choice made by myself hopefully in her best interests but nonetheless a painful choice to make. I have to be honest and say that my transition is part of why I have let her go, she was not developing, I felt in a normal way. Not wanting to bring friends home, not being able to interact with me naturally, our interaction all seemed so stunted. Its still early days and we are going through the learning process, I make sure to the best of my ability that they retain all their 'choices' of who to tell and when to tell and what to tell. For my part I try and consider them in the choices I make which will affect them in some way, but to be honest the real big ones are yet to come.

The weddings, the in-laws, the grandchildren, etc., for instance I feel that I have no role to play at my children's weddings, I am not the father of the groom, one already exists elsewhere, I am not the father of the bride, as I already said one exists elsewhere and I am certainly not the 'mother in law. So to some degree I have sacrificed my parental position to live the life I have chosen, my children may in fact make a choice that there is no place for me at all at their weddings, though I hope this is not the case. Time will tell on this issue and the multitude that are to follow.

As I said already we are all on a learning curve and only time and patience can work through the current and future issues. As long as the communication lines stay open, we as a family can have empathy for each other, mutual respect and a lot of love, we will keep working together as a unit.

Many of the extended family I told by letter, the family you only see at weddings and funerals. I told them out of courtesy and none replied, nephews and nieces I told personally, which went down reasonably well. The younger generation seem to be more accepting of diversity, though the questions came thick and fast and we had many a laugh about the effects of the transition process.

At family events which have occurred since I became visibly male and of course that I have been invited to attend, I have been treated well. Some of the looks from people I don't know from Adam, have been evidence that the grapevine once again was working well, but at least I was invited and it's starting to be old news now, at last.

It's taken some time for them to realize that I am no different now than I was before, it's only the exterior that has changed to match my internal gender identity. The family recollections of stories which make you laugh to the point where your eyes stream with tears are still just as funny, I haven't disowned them or the life that I led before. I feel to deny who I was denies who I have become. Although just occasionally family and friends go just a little too far and press that big red button inside me which wants to forget how I lived as a female and yes, there are things I wish to forget.

All in all I think my family have risen to the challenge of having a trans person in their midst rather well and for that they all deserve a pat on the back. No door is closed to me and mine and you can't ask for more than that, though I must say I do draw the line at joining my nephews for a piss up on a stag night at the local dive, the point is though - I was invited.

2004 Picture of me with a Wedding cake I had made for my nephew, this is something I do only for the family these days

Me aged 24 and two of my children.

My wedding day first time round,
with the dress I made for myself.

A Fairy Story explaining transsexualism to young children, kindly donated for publication in this book by Mr. Tom Wallis.

Some parents may feel that a fairy story is not the best way of explaining facts to children and that may be a valid comment. I would draw the reader therefore to G.I.R.E.S. website where a worksheet is available to explain the facts to perhaps older children.

ONE DAY, A LONG TIME ago in baby land, where the fairies make the babies a sad mistake was about to happen. The fairies who were normally very careful little folk, took great care to get things right. To make a baby they would carefully find a girl's brain, filled with all the right thoughts and feelings for a little girl and then match it with a girls body, these would fit together perfectly for the rest of the babies life. The same care would be given to matching up little boy's brains with little boys bodies, so they could be happy with how they thought and felt for the rest of their lives.

On this particular day the fairies had been working very hard for a very long time. Bella who was the fairy that was to make this mistake was very tired and it was nearly time to go home. Poor Bella had been rushing around all day and she thought she has just enough time to make one more baby. A pretty little girl, she thought to herself because she had been working on boys all day. Off she rushed not thinking what she was doing and picked up a boys brain, as she had been doing all day. Then she dashed up the aisle and collected a girl's body, as she picked it up the bell rang to end her days work. In her rush to get home Bella forgot the normal checks she should make and placed the brain in the body. There was a lot of noise of fairies and elves going home so Bella did not hear the warning buzzer that at any other time would have warned of a mistake. Bella grabbed a box, labelled the baby for delivery and went off home rather happy with her days work. Her mistake was to cause years of misery and worry, but it would not be discovered for a very long time.

Many years passed and the little girl was very uncomfortable with herself, she just could not do what her parents wanted, she was not a little girl who wanted to play house or with dolls. She wanted to climb trees and play football and with her brothers toys. This little girl was starting to grow up and now life became even more difficult, her body was changing but not how she thought it should. It was betraying her and becoming a woman's body instead of a mans. The man inside, was making the woman's body very uncomfortable. Her upbringing made her think she should get married and have children just like any normal person. She tried hard to do this and made the man she married very sad and the children confused as she was doing the dads role of playing football and other manly things. Sadly the marriage ended in divorce.

It took several years to discover that there were other people out there who felt the same and were as uncomfortable with themselves as this person was and they had information that this person needed.

There are some special doctors who tried to make the mans brain feel more comfortable in the woman's body but this made the mans brain even more unhappy. These doctors seemed to be sure that the brain was wrong but they did not quite know how it was wrong so they could not fix it.

One day the man found out about another type of doctor who knew even more people who seemed to have the wrong brain and who understood about how sometimes the wrong brains get into the wrong bodies. More strangely still he had met other people just like this contused person, sometimes it was a mans brain in a woman's body but there were also women's brains in men's bodies.

This doctor knew how to fix the people who came to him. He knew that there was no chance of changing the brain so the best thing for these people was to make the body fit what the brain said it was. When he was told this, the man inside the woman's body was so happy. he was not the only person like this and the mistake the fairy made all those years ago could be fixed.

The doctor did the fixing that was needed for the man and he was so much happier with how he felt. He could finally come and live in the world how he felt he should, and better still no longer shouted quite so much at the people who lived around him.

A few years have passed since this wonderful doctor started to make the changes that would make the outer woman's body look like the mans body that the brain has known all along that it is, but the changes that have so far happened have made the man so much happier that he can live a normal life and feel as if he is part of the human race at last.

Needless to say that the security measures in baby land have been altered so that these mistakes happen less often but they do still happen sometimes. Someone you know could be on of those mistakes and they need your help and understanding to help them cope.

The man this mistake happened to now lives a happy contented life with a wonderful partner, two very understanding children and two wonderful grandchildren who know and accept that their granddad is a man who used to be their mummies mummy. Who said children don't take things in their stride? To them granddad is just a third granddad but a little different to the other two.

Tom Wallis.

TRANSMAN

Relationships

THROUGHOUT THIS BOOK I HAVE mentioned relationships but feel this subject needs a section of its own to give it justice. Relationships after all are a fundamental necessity for most people, who really wants to live alone?

At one point in my transition after my five and a half year relationship failed, as a direct result of my choice to transition, I resigned myself, not reluctantly but realistically, to the prospect of spending the rest of my natural alone.

I really do feel that it cannot be easy for someone, male or female, to enter into a relationship with a trans person. The choice they make for themselves not only affects them but they are making a choice for their family also.

Although we like to kid ourselves that we can melt away, post transition, into society the reality is often far from the fantasy and trans, or being trans, somehow always plays a part in our lives.

I freely admit that I have reached the point in my own life where I forget that I am trans, a person of transsexual origin, a transman, and it comes as a shock when I am outed.

A year or so ago I was delivering training to a group of student nurses on HIV prevention and as part of that training I asked the students if they had made any assumptions about my HIV status. I was rocked to the core when one of them said "not about your HIV status but I think you used to be a woman".

I was unable to continue on with the training, not because of my own shock at the statement but because the whole group responded with a gasp. I could not lie to them and the 'elephant in the room that everybody now knew was there but didn't want to acknowledge' had to be dealt with. I had no choice but to suspend the HIV training and allow a ten minute question time on trans.

The point I am trying to make is that although we get on with our lives, trans follows us about, just waiting to rear its head and for a partner to join us in a relationship they need to understand the implications of the decision they are making for themselves and their family.

For someone to consider coming into my life 'till death us do part' and all that, is made more complex by the fact I put myself out in the public eye. This is via training and the work I do with Trans-Shropshire, in an effort to educate the public in some small way around trans issues.

If I am well known and visible as a trans person then my partner will be visible also, with the potential risk of becoming a target for transphobic attacks herself and other possible complications.

I feel that to talk to a potential partner about the choice she/he is making is the only way forward. I am not saying that's how other people should deal with it, but I do need to know that someone is thinking carefully about their choice to pair up with me and not just drifting into it on a wave of emotion.

If I am honest, there are many reasons for feeling this way and some of them are because my long term and stable relationship failed as a result of my transitioning. Even though I know that was because their sexuality was being threatened by me becoming visibly male. There's no getting away from the fact we learn from our mistakes, I hope, and I do not want to be in that situation again, for my benefit or my partners benefit. I would rather we spoke sooner than later and made an educated choice, not an emotional choice.

Call me clinical if you wish, it's the way I do things and it works for me.

Some of the assumptions I have come across from partners have been interesting to say the least. They assume that because I used to be female then I will understand their every needs, want and desire. That's just simply not true! Women are just as much a mystery to me as to any other man and it's compounded by the fact they think I should understand and I don't.

I am supposed to like shopping – I hate shopping. I am supposed to be totally understanding of how to stimulate a woman – I haven't got a clue though am learning all the time! If I make a comment which for some reason is deemed as sexist I'm told I should know better, one example of this is as follows.

My current partner had a problem with her washing machine, not ours, hers, she had it before I met her. So I offered to buy her another one as a gift which she was very happy about. That night we went to the pub and sat with a few female friends and we started talking about this new all singing and dancing washing machine and I said that I had bought it for her as a present. I thought they where going to lynch me, "you don't buy a woman a washing machine you buy them flowers" was snarled at me and "you should no better with your history" was thrown at me. All I could do was sit there and feel what happened? did I do something wrong, if so what the fuck was it because I couldn't see what the fuss was about. The woman needed a washing machine and I bought her one as a gift – end of story.

The sex aspect of relationships I feel has been covered by the 'Sex Stuff' chapter within this book and I do not wish to go over ground I have already explained. So if you take sex out of the equation what components are left within a relationship?

The one that come to mind is friendship first and foremost, if we cannot make a friend of our partner then how can we truly communicate. Surely our partner should also be our best friend.

The next point that would come to mind is companionship, having some-one to share life's ups and downs, to travel with to Bognor or Bangkok, what ever your preference is. To have a companion, who is also your friend, would be a wonderful place to be in a relationship.

Other desirable qualities within a relationship could be listed but this would be an endless list and really what we need to know is what we actually want or expect from a partner.

What I would like to see in my ideal partner would be companionship to enjoy life's ups and support each other in life's downs. Mutual respect for each other, equality with neither partner feeling they are better than the other, different strengths and weaknesses yes, but equal nonetheless.

To get the above list ticked in every box may be a task in itself however I find myself at this point in my life in the happy position of having all my boxes ticked.

I am nearly three years into a relationship with a wonderful woman. Someone who has raised a family as have I, who has been married as have I and has had her own home. We are equals in most things though our strengths and weaknesses are different.

We are like chalk and cheese but does that matter? Not at all, because if you have mutual respect you accept each others differences and as a unit that makes you even richer.

In 2006 and we hope to be married, once I have been able to obtain my new birth certificate as a result of the Gender Recognition Act and I sincerely hope that we have a long and happy future together.

I think I would like to make one more point on relationships and that is we have no right to judge others and the relationships they choose for themselves.

Being trans is diverse with a capital D and no two trans people will have the same experience.

Many choose an open relationship with one or the other having many partners. Some choose not to go into a relationship at all and believe me are happy to be alone, living full and rewarding lives in their own way at their own pace.

The real issue once again is choice, almost everything comes back to choice. If we choose to be in a relationship then that's fine, if we choose not to be in a relationship that is also fine, each to their own as they say and good luck to them all.

Top Right: Jayne whilst we were on holiday in Fuertaventura 2003
Bottom left: Miss Shagwell & Austin Powers ready for a night on the town.

TRANSMAN

A Partner's Perspective

I WAS ASKED IF I WOULD write something for this section of this book by Rico - as his partner.

I feel that to place things into perspective I have no choice but to write this from ALL angles, to assist where possible in giving an insight just what it is like to live with trans issues when you are not a trans individual yourself.

Up until 2000 the only information I had about Transsexualism was what I had gleaned from the media - television, radio, newspaper stories and magazine articles I had read. I was a stereotypical heterosexual raised by the same type of parents, if it didn't affect me directly I didn't have the need to find out, it was just curiosity or a talking point in conversation where much of the information banded about was incorrect or supposition. All that changed - in a BIG way.

In the Beginning

I met Rico in 2002 through an ex-partner (whom I do not wish to discuss). I found him warm, intelligent and rather good looking - I found his goatee quite sexy too. I knew I liked him from the very beginning - but attracted to him? Well, to be honest I was and I wasn't. I was attracted to his qualities rather than his physical characteristics, admittedly, he wasn't my usual type!

In the past I generally went for a guy around 5'10"-6', sporty build, clean shaven, hands like shovels, feet like boats, and hair, hair is good as long as it's in the right places (grey is ok as long as it was only a tiny bit), not down the back/over the shoulders, 'Gorillas in the Mist' is a fantastic film - but I didn't really want a primate in my bathroom if you know what I mean?

Where body hair is concerned, Rico could put a Yeti to shame if it was around 5ft nothing, got small feet/hands, going bald with a bit of a tummy, and you know what? I must have been quite a bit shallow before because what you may have found amusing just now - I find it quite sexy after 2 1/2 years of living with Rico and wouldn't change a dammed thing (except for maybe his feet - lets not go there!).

Working it Through

No one said it would be easy, least of all Rico. He made sure I was fully aware of his past, present and future plans for himself regarding his transition, and we discussed fully what we hoped our future had in store for us - at the beginning we had no idea that marriage would be on the horizon. I would be lying to you if I said our relationship is perfect, though it's as close as it's going to get. But hey, what relationship is perfect, both of you have to work at it - and sometimes it's bloody hard work from both points of view, transition is just another issue you work through together, it's important to do this if the relationship is to have any future at all. At the time of writing this section of the book, we have 6 adult children and 1 under 16 from past relationships on both sides and going on 4 grandchildren under 10. We work dammed hard, generally too shattered to go out till all hours on a frequent basis like we used to and can get a little antagonistic with each other at times - much to the amusement of one of our friends, who finds our petty differences of opinions VERY funny indeed.

Being There

I have fully supported Rico in whatever choices he has made for himself regarding his transition processes, his happiness is just as important to me as my own. I have seen him in pain after surgery (both chest and abdominal) and done what I can to make his recovery less traumatic. I have been as supportive as I am able over his children and have tried to care for them as though they were my own (though this has been difficult at times and I dare say he will ditto my thoughts regarding my own children). I was behind him 110% when he wanted to set up Trans-Shropshire, helped out by working 5 days in the office and a number of evenings and bought work home at weekends for over a year (all voluntary). I assisted him in setting up the Gender Advisory Bureau, for 6months it was voluntary then became paid employment as the work came in. I have also seen him collapse with what appeared to be a stroke and the subsequent 6 weeks recovery period needed to heal himself. I have worried for him when he talks of further surgery - just like the other times, but I know he will never take risks, he educates himself and if it's appears too risky then it isn't happening.

Your Place or Mine?

Sex can be a little awkward at times, for both of us.

In the beginning I had never been with a trans guy that had used a prosthetic penis before and when I saw the size of it, to say that I was a little unsure of how I would cope is perhaps an understatement (laughs). For one I hadn't had regular sex with a guy for a while, for another, although Rico's penis looks the business, it fits into a harness and has an attachment that vibrates with a wire hanging down and a control box. I fully understood the functions of each piece and why it was there but that first time we had sex - I felt like a virgin all over again, apart from position and movement, everything else was new to me and I was very nervous. I needn't have worried though, Rico told me that if there was anything that I didn't like or was uncomfortable with that he would stop. So, armed with all this knowledge and experience with a couple of men from past long term relationships, I thought 'hey, go for it!' We were going at it for a while, things were progressing just fine, then he switched on his device. Now I have never really been one for vibrators, have one but had to take the batteries out because the noise and sensation puts me off when I am trying to reach climax, I actually don't like vibrators at all, certainly not for pleasure more out of total need when I was single. So, Rico pumps up the vibration, I feel it but most of all - I hear it above our own noises, and I am unable to climax. We talked about it at the time and have had the same thing happen a few times since but not that often for it to be a major problem.

I remember the first time I asked to see Rico's real penis, or rather his micro penis. You know I couldn't stop smiling, not because I found it funny or even mildly amusing, but because I was amazed, amazed that male hormones had that sort of effect on female genitalia but also amazed that it looked (please excuse the pun) every inch just like a, well like a penis is supposed to, only much smaller than what I had seen before. Also, when aroused, there seems to be so much more penis inside the body that is held back by anatomy, and upon standing upright at this point, it becomes almost twice as large again as when laying down - gravity does very strange things at times.

Because I could actually see a penis and not what used to be a clitoris, I attempted oral sex and found it not that bad under the circumstances, the only thing was that it was a little close to other regions of Rico's anatomy that neither of us want me to go, but with Rico's direction I have mastered it now and is second nature so to speak.

Dealing with the Crap

I myself have had varying forms of hassle while with trans partners, and because of my work. My sexuality has been questioned a number of times (which has become rather boring), I have been told that I should be put against the wall and shot along with the weirdoes I work with, I have been told that my marriage in 2006 to the man I love will never be accepted by certain individuals within the family (although it is lawful), have been stared at, pointed at, gossiped about and I feel tolerated rather than accepted by the local LGB community, and to be honest - though it stinks and has become very tedious, I accept that there will always be people out there with narrow minded opinions they want to tell me about, but they are not going to stop or scare me into not working with the trans community if I wish to, or from being in that space, or prevent me from loving my partner. If they don't like it, all they have to do is look away.

My Family - Friend or Foe?

I had already told my kids about Rico before we began our relationship. To be honest, when I told them that we were in a relationship the only one that seemed surprised was me, but they had no objections whatsoever as they quite liked him anyway. My daughter and youngest son tend to call Rico 'Dad' when they're after a favour or something (a little emotional blackmail I think - laughs), the rest of the time just like their elder brother, they call him Ric and are generally respectful toward him. To my grandchildren he's simply Granddad/Granddad Ric (in my grandson's case) or Gandalf (because my Granddaughter can't say Granddad). In fact when we marry, all our children and grandchildren have important roles to play on the day, each and every one of them are fully included and as such are as much a party to the day as Rico and I are.

When I told the only member of my siblings I have contact with (my brother - whom I trust) about Rico being a trans guy, Rico wasn't impressed at all, not so much that I told him but because I didn't ask Rico if it was ok. I learn very quick even though I meant no disrespect. My brother was absolutely fine about it, he had spent much of his life in the forces in Germany and now lives in Spain, European way of life is so much more laid back than in Britain. My bro did say a couple of things though which made me smile "Ain't your bloke got diddy feet for a geezer, an e's 'airy aint he!" that was before I told him our news (I didn't tell him because of the comment), then afterward he looked at me stunned at first, then smiled "you're avin a laff, wot you on about, Ric's got a beard!", I said that was down to the male hormones to which he replied "Well Jayne, all I see is a bloke, and there is nothing about that bloke that says anything remotely female to me, I've been in the forces with plenty of blokes for a number of years an some of them I wouldn't go the toilet with, but tell you what though, I wouldn't ave any problem at all goin the toilet with Ric, and as long as he treats you right, then he's right with me!". At this point I thanked him for the sentiment, told him to shut up and shoved another bottled beer in his hand - bless him and all that type of macho bulls**t. Seriously though, when I asked my brother if he would come over from Spain when we get married and give me away, apart from saying that he would be honoured, he comes out with another gem "bin trying to give you away for 40 odd years Jayne!" - funny bro, very funny!

His wife knows now, as does his adult daughter and her partner, no issues, no problems, they laugh and joke, they accept that this is the way it is and they welcome Rico into their side of the family. Makes me feel kind of warm somehow, especially as they never had much, if any, contact with my previous partners.

Final Bit

In bringing this section to a close, there was much more I could have said and that I wanted to say, especially as Rico threw down the gauntlet to me to do it. I could have told you some good, bad and ugly stories I hear in my course of work with trans people/families, about things like hate crime, surgery gone wrong, self mutilation and problems with funding for treatments, it isn't all good out there at all. But I think the 4 pages I have typed up are more than Rico expected anyway. _

This main section was written in the hope that I have given you an insight into what it's like for me, living with a man of Transsexual origin.

Now I write for the guys (or girls) out there, who may live with someone like myself. We know you have dreams for your future, to aspire to be the men (women) that you are. We support and care for you as you do for us, but just as you lived your lives in the shadow of others for many years and needed to shine in your own right, do not get so caught up with what you want/need that you become so like the takers from your past. Do not forget your present/future givers - they have dreams too and wish to shine also. For you to 'give a damn', is that you remember how it felt to always place your own wants and needs second, remember not to be selfish in your hopes and dreams for the future, keep the relationship inclusive with open/honest communication between you and hopefully find true equality with your partner.

TRANSMAN

What's In A Name...?

I WAS BORN AND ASSIGNED THE sex of female. I was named by my father who saw only a female infant put before him, and the name he chose for me was Helen Marie Thompson.

The name we are given is the choice of our parents, the surname of course usually follows the father, in the U.K, unless the mother is not married or the biological father is unknown due to A.I. or other conception means. We have precious little choice of how we are labelled at birth, either in name or sex, but as adults we can make that choice for ourselves and change our name legally to reflect that choice.

I had most of my life felt uncomfortable with my birth name and I really can't be sure whether that was a gender thing or just I didn't agree with my parents taste. Once my gender reassignment process was under way I chose to do something at last about the name and was faced with what name to pick for myself.

As a teenager I had adopted a couple of nick names, the one I will tell you about shortly the other I will mention now.

The first name I remember being chosen for me at school was 'butcher' because my mother made me wear a stripy apron every time I walked out of the door. Others used by the local kids where versions of my surname i.e. 'tomcat' and 'tom tom'. However the first name I chose for myself was a pseudonym, namely Sam Ducket.

Me aged 3

Now the interesting thing about this name was what went along with it and that was the beginnings of exploring a male identity.

I was about 13 maybe 14 years old when I started to tell strangers my name was Sam, I told them that I had been born a boy and altered surgically to be a girl and that I hated it – all lies and more lies. The only things wrong with me at birth was that my thumbs went the wrong way , I didn't have a coccyx bone at the bottom of my spine and I was supposedly born a 'blue baby', according to my mother, something about her being a Rhesus negative blood group ??

I went further with the name of Sam and even started to build another life almost. Travelling out of the little town of Wenlock to Shrewsbury and getting up to all kinds of mischief in the name of Sammy Ducket. Somewhere in the dark recesses of a police filling system is a police record for Sammy Ducket and on that subject I will say no more.

I mentioned earlier about having another nick name from when I was a teenager, believe it or not that's all down to Barry Manilow who sang that song Copacabana back in the seventies. That picture he painted of Rico wearing a diamond, a high flyer and a guy who had the eye for the ladies was just too good to waste. So when it came to changing my name officially it seemed logical to try and adopt that name 'Rico' for my own identity. Much to the scorn of friends and disgust of family who insisted that I was calling my self 'Ricardo'.

The name Rico also spoke to me of Spanish blood, passion, romance and lazy sunny days. None of which I had (well maybe passion and romance) but one can fantasize these things and for years that's all my life really was, a dream of what it could be, a fantasy of how I wanted to be.

Rico or Rick is also a break down of the name Richard, a good solid English name, you recall Richard the Lion heart and all that historical stuff. No there was no doubt about it, my first name had to be Rico whether people liked it or not, so best foot forward, caution to the wind, I settled on this name and made it my own.

The second name I chose for myself was Adrian, another good solid name and one I had been drawn to for most of my life. Yet to have this as my first name was not flamboyant enough, Adrian had to go second.

My surname was a hard choice and one I was thinking about for a couple of years. I did not want to betray my family heritage by leaving behind Thompson, the family name, but it really didn't feel appropriate to stick with that name. If I was going to start a new chapter in my life I wanted to do it in style and my surname had to fit.

I remember my mother saying that I should take my fathers name, Leonard Thompson, but this felt very uncomfortable, taking the name of my father, the man my mother had been married to for 30 years or so. I was uncomfortable and unwilling to go down that road at all.

I eventually settled on Paris for many reasons. One reason was the very place Paris, the capital of France, a place I had been to many times and loved, a place full of old and new, amazing architecture, museums, rich in history, a place I felt at home. Another reason was mythology and the legend of Troy with the dashing Paris and the Helen of Troy stories, Paris was an ancient name and as I am so often accused, I like 'olden days' things.

The final reason was down to Star-Trek, the futuristic vision of life from many worlds all living together in one community. The diversity of many races all working together and the character of Tom Paris a slightly renegade and independent member of the crew of Voyager, the ship that went where none had gone before. Yes, Paris was the name I chose for my surname and in 2000 it became my legally adopted title.

I had contemplated changing my name well before I made a choice to transition, about a year and a half before to be honest. I remember that my partner at that time and I had decided to have a child and prior to his birth my partner changed her name so that our child would carry the name of Paris. This was because my circumstances were still complex and I could not live full-time the way I wanted to. We felt that if the child had my surname all set up, when the time came for me to change my name we would all fit together nicely as a family unit. Grand plans but all to no avail as the relationship eventually failed anyway.

Changing your name is a relatively simple process, you can change it in several legal ways, I chose to change mine by 'Statutory Declaration', I remember typing it all out myself and going to see the solicitor to make it all official but that's when the real fun starts.

People don't always realize the full extent of changing not only your name but your gender identity on paperwork, it can be a nightmare, I remember drawing up a grand plan of action trying to get the official notifications off in a sequence which would not cause too many problems.

I had to change my passport, have my National Insurance number coded to protect my past identity, I had to change bank details, utility bills, and much more. The two most difficult were the passport and driving license, not because they objected to my change of name or gender but simply because I had to change them so early in my transition and they were both forms of photo I.D. I was not convincing as a man at that point and trying to get a macho looking photo was a tough task. The passport was not too bad I got pleasantly pissed and put a leather coat on sneaking into Tesco's at

2 in the morning, hoping to God that nobody saw me. The driving license was appalling, but that's par for the course I'm afraid.

I remember when I changed my details at the Family Credit office I was given the option of being Ms, Miss, Mrs., Dr, or Reverend Rico Adrian Paris, the only viable option was Reverend however seeing as I was not a man of the cloth it was totally unacceptable. The way they got round it was to have the payment book made up by hand rather than processed automatically, funny situation to find yourself in.

I started off this section by saying 'What's in a name?' Well as you can see from the above paragraphs, for me there is a lot in a name. I wanted to pick something that told people something about who I was as a person, that captured my personality and I feel I achieved that with my choice.

Others keep their surnames, or choose a Christian name similar to their previous birth name. For me there was no way this was going to be a viable option, to be honest I had been looking for a way of dropping the names I had been given for years, although it sounds like a grand plan honestly it was not. However, it was a great opportunity to reshape the perceived image of the person I was, by changing the most personal of labels given to us in society, ones own name.

TRANSMAN

Counselling

Now IF ONE SUBJECT STIRS up feelings and thoughts (no pun intended) when it comes to people of transsexual origin it's that of counselling and psychotherapy. I feel this is partly because of the association in peoples minds that trans is a mental health issue when it is not and the fact a psychiatrist has to make a diagnosis of transsexualism in the first place.

Although transsexualism is not a declarable mental health illness there is no getting away from the fact that to transition from one gender to another does bring a phenomenal number of stressful situations and issues. These may lead to people needing to go into a period of counselling to help sort, sift and file the information, clear their minds of the clutter, to move forward with choices and live full and rewarding lives.

Also currently in the UK, counselling and psychotherapy are recommended in the 'Harry Benjamin Criteria '(no minimum or maximum number of sessions) and so for many people, therapy is an essential part of the early stages of transition. Especially if they are going through the National Health Service route to obtain treatment as opposed to the Private route where therapy is often, sadly I feel, over looked.

I have an interest in Counselling and Psychotherapy from two stances, the first being of course the professional side of things, being a Psychotherapist my self, and chalking up over 288 hours of one to one work in the last year alone, working with a variety of patients exploring aspects of GID.

The second book in a series of three I wish to write is 'Counselling the Trans Client – Bite size', giving several case studies of the presenting issue and how we worked through that issue. This book will be aimed at counsellors who wish to understand more about transsexualism, transgender and transvestism to the mutual benefit of their own professional development and the all important process of helping clients through this extraordinary complex stage in development.

The second interest is a personal one, my own history. When it comes to counselling and psychiatric evaluation it has been a rocky road and a major reason why I initially chose to go down the private route to transition in the first place.

So lets start by looking at the professional aspect of my thoughts on counselling and really I have to start with my progress towards becoming a Gender & Sexuality therapist in the first place. If I am honest this is something that had been thrust upon me, not in a bad way, simply the way things evolved because of working as a volunteer in different ways within the LGBT. community in Shropshire for the past nine years or more.

I was approached by people who had nobody to share personal issues with. People who needed to talk and used social occasions to explore private situations. I found that people were able to talk to me and open up about these life issues for whatever reason and the more it happened the more I felt a responsibility to have some kind of training in counselling skills or listening skills so that I was equipt to help in any way I could.

Eventually I took a part-time 'Introduction to Counselling' course which gave me a taster of what was required from a therapist and this fuelled my desire to enrol for more appropriate training.

I studied for two years in Birmingham with a group of similarly minded people and learned Person Centred and Gestalt therapeutic models. After completing and gaining a vocational qualification in Counselling I eventually took a Diploma in Psychotherapy, passing with distinction. At last feeling that I had taken my responsibility to potential clients seriously and acted accordingly in equipping myself in dealing with whatever problems clients chose to bring into the therapeutic relationship, pertaining to sexuality or gender identity.

I was lucky enough to secure a position within a sexual health service organisation and worked with 'men who had sex with men' for three years.

I co-founded and worked with 'Woman 2 Woman' for three years, a project which dealt with issues faced by women who had sex with women or who where questioning their gender identity and it was during this period I commenced working with trans individuals.

By the time I commenced writing this book I was working mainly with clients exploring gender identity, via Trans-Shropshire. Though I have retained my placement with the sexual health service provider and continue to work with Gay/Bi men as and when required.

Working with GID is a fascinating and rewarding occupation. Clearly I had to firstly identify my own buttons or sensitivities, so that during therapy other peoples experiences did not stir up my own baggage, and the two years training I went through equipped me well towards this end.

Some people have mentioned to me concerns about a person of trans-sexual origin working as a therapist for clients having trans issues, that possibly I am too close to the subject. These individuals are correct in raising this issue because it is a very important one, however the training you receive, if it is good training, will teach you that identifying your own buttons is paramount and then learning to bracket off those feelings for yourself when those buttons are pressed. To take any issues or sensitivities of your own to Supervision is an essential part of working as a counsellor or psychotherapist. If necessary take counselling yourself, whilst giving therapy to others, is best practice.

It is very important to be constantly aware of assumptions we may or may not make when working with a client, if you have personal experience within your own life of those same or similar issues. By making assump-tions about our clients we detract from the clients own experience and at the end of the day that is the reason for a person entering therapy in the first place, to explore their own issues and not yours.

As a therapist it is important to continue your training, we never will reach a stage in our professional lives when we know everything there is to know about a person, people are all different, our experiences affect us all in different ways, it is important also to be guided by an ethical frame-work as a practicing Counsellor. For myself I adhere to that of the British Association of Counsellors & Psychotherapist.

On to the second reason for being interested in the subject of counselling as mentioned previously and this is of course my own personal experience.

I was very reluctant to go into counselling in any shape or form prior to my transition, the reason being I had been in various forms of therapy, on and off, since my teenage years and on each and every occasion my feelings were not listened to. I was not heard, and was encouraged to 'make do' with my life.

I found it very challenging to go and see yet another psychiatrist for a diagnosis. I had a distrust of anyone or anything linked with mental or psychological health. The only way forward for me was to try and take control of the situation and choose my own psychiatrist, make my own arrangements and retain all my options and choices all along the path to diagnosis.

There is no doubt about the fact 'control' was something important to me and has been a leading thread running throughout my transition. However, this is clearly due to the fact I had lived 37 years of a life that had been so out of control and influenced by everyone else except me.

I did keep all those around me informed about what I intended to do including my doctor who supported my choice, she agreed to be led by the Consultant Psychiatrist when it came to implementing my transition, and this is indeed what happened.

I still do have a big red button and am very wary of anyone who works with me, in relation to me and my own transition, from a psychiatric or psychological stance. To be honest I do not think that button will ever go away. The good thing is, of course, that I am self aware enough to identify this button and am aware when it's pressed and why it's pressed. Also when my clients are expressing the same kind of feeling I am able to empathize with them, though self disclosure is of course inappropriate and I would therefore not tell them this is how I felt too when I first transitioned.

No matter how we feel there is no getting away from the reality of transitioning from one gender into another and the implications it has on our health and well-being. I feel that psychotherapy and counselling are important in providing a safe space to let the emotions and feelings out, to explore them and eventually let them go. Lets face it, sometimes two heads are better than one in finding solutions to life's challenges, possibly broadening out our options through therapy. As long as the therapist remembers our choices will always remain our choices and it is not for someone else to thrust their wishes upon us.

TRANSMAN

Emotions - A Minefield

EMOTIONS - WHAT ARE THEY?

Well I think this is one of those questions that each one of us would answer very differently depending upon our own life experiences. Perhaps what we have studied academically and maybe what kind of relationships have shaped us and how emotions have played a part in our lives would affect our answer.

You could say that emotions are what set us apart from other animals, though that is debatable, emotions are what makes us different from robots definitely and the very essence of being 'human'.

For me emotions have been the bane of my existence most of my life and as a result have fuelled me through many years of reflection, ever learning new ways to express or more often, how to control them. Sometimes, even controlling them too much, to the point of being seen as an 'inner control freak'.

At this point I could break down the stages in my life and analyse the fuck out of how I got to where I am now emotionally. By sharing with you that as an adolescent emotions affected me like this, or, in my twenties emotions affected me like that, but that's not really what I want to do in this book. Talking about where I am now and the effect of transitioning on my emotions is perhaps more apt and so that's what I will try to focus on.

Quite simply if I am feeling, I cannot think. Using logic or thinking things through is how I function best in my life. So I take the controlling of my emotions seriously because at the end of the day I want to think, not feel. Perhaps I'm a budding 'Spock'.

I'm not a stone, I do feel emotion, like anyone else, if someone I care about is hurting I will hurt too. If someone or something hurts me I feel the pain, I love, I laugh, I feel envy, I feel anger, you name the emotion and I have it too. However, I choose to control how I show it and that often means the people around me see me as a bit of a mystery, hard to interact with or talk to.

I have had people try and push me to react and see at what point I do get angry or cry, telling me that I am like a machine and have no feelings. At the time it was a bit of an eye opener and hurtful but I dealt with the hurt I felt as I always do, by talking about it, not displaying the emotion of the hurt.

When I started my male hormones my biggest worry was that I would become emotionally unstable in the way I had been in my twenties. That period in my life was a rollercoaster and I was always physically drained from emotional issues, issues I could not resolve.

People annoyed the heck out of me in my twenties and I became quite reclusive except for well structured interaction with others such as through religious meetings. My relationship at that age bore the brunt of my flooding, uncontrollable, ups and downs, the pendulum swinging from physically hitting my partner to emotionally torturing them and more.

When I look back on how I behaved towards the person I shared my life with and had children with, I feel very ashamed, however what good does it do to hold on to the wrongs of our past? We cannot change the past and our prior deeds, we can only learn from them and strive to become a better person now and in the future.

It took many years to recognise and control my behaviour and become a reasonable person to be around rather than a two headed tiger. When I started my masculinising hormones I was so scared of taking a leap back in time to the person I had been. Especially as I was told that one of the side effects of the sustanon was an increased risk of being aggressive/volatile.

The consultant I saw for my prescribed hormones was the only person I chose to share this with and they gave me a good bit of advice, he said to me "We all have emotions but we also have the ability to control those emotions if we choose to" The word I picked up on there was CHOOSE and have remembered his words of wisdom daily since.

Yes my emotions may fluctuate due to massive doses of hormones being injected into my backside but in my hand remains the control of how to deal with it. I could if I wished show it, hide it, channel it, ignore it or get to the root of the cause of it. This I could do by distracting myself, talking about the issue, taking myself out of the situation, analyzing why I felt the emotion, getting advice about it, share it with my friends or even seek therapy if it was that bad, etc. etc.

Time and again I see clients come my way who are emotionally on a roller coaster after recently starting hormones, either MtF or FtM, and I understand where they are. It is very important to remember this phase does pass and for some people it never happens at all.

It seems in my experience, if there is a predisposition to mild or moderate depression then this can be an indicator that the hormones may and I stress may, make you low within a few weeks after starting them. The key factor is to remember there is a reason for being low and that in time it will pass. Whilst feeling low its best to keep a balanced life, work, rest and play, eat well, sleep well and keep life as uncomplicated as possible, pamper yourself until it passes.

On the flip side of the above I have also seen those that have a tendency to self-harm or feel suicidal, which is alleviated by starting hormones. So the emotions can fluctuate for the good as well as the not so good. Each person is different and it is not possible to accurately predict the effects of hormones on any one person.

I do feel there is another important point to remember and that's transitioning from one gender to another is not the cure for all life's problems.

By this I mean if you had lived a life of poor physical health prior to transition, changing your gender will not necessarily cure your health problems, or if you had money problems or housing issues prior to transitioning, changing gender will not cure your finances or get you a new home.

I see regularly people who believe that changing from one gender to another will end all life's problems and the truth is that life's problems remain. You, as an individual, may feel better within yourself, may have a higher self-esteem or levels of confidence. In short you may have a more fulfilling life in the gender you believe yourself to be by being true to yourself and showing the world by visibly transitioning, but changing gender is not a magic cure all.

It is important to consider our emotional health along with our mental health and general well being when we take the road to change our gender via hormones and surgery. The journey is challenging, with many ups and downs along the way – pace yourself and if it's meant to be it will happen for you.

TRANSMAN

Volunteering – A Big Part Of My Life

I STARTED IN 1987, FULL OF zeal, motivated, energized and raring to go.

Back then, which feels like a hundred ago, I wanted to be a volunteer, not for trans folk at that time but for people who struggled with bladder and kidney problems. As mentioned earlier I struggled with bladder and kidney problems all of my 'sexually active with men' period in life, to the point where I became desperate for support and none was available.

At that time my GP was very supportive and said why not turn some of that negative frustration into something useful and set up a support group of my own? Seemed a damn good idea to me and so I set about the task of turning my utility room into an office and bombarding anyone and everyone with letters for support, financial or in kind.

Eventually I set up a local branch of the National Kidney Research Fund in Shrewsbury, had a launch with the local Mayor, went on local radio for a live interview and my home was bombarded with letters from fellow sufferers in Shropshire.

After a couple of years I walked away from the Chair position, due to my marital breakdown but left behind me a strong support group which I hope still runs today. What I did take away with me though was a tried and tested way of setting up a support group. A system I have used time and again throughout my 18 years of working as a volunteer and one I can share with others to replicate IF they want to set something up themselves.

Firstly, if you are considering setting up some kind of support provision for others you need to be aware of your own limitations.

Believe me when I say that volunteering is challenging, time consuming and at times draining though clearly it can be rewarding and even therapeutic in some circumstances.

You will find that there are many people who wish to volunteer but very few who can drive an idea forward or commit to long term involvement, come hell or high water. If you are looking for gratitude – you won't get it, if you are looking for reliability from other volunteers – expect none, anything else is a bonus! If you are thinking that a couple of hours a week is all you will need to put in – you're deluding yourself, its more likely to be 7 days a week at times.

If you the reader want to volunteer, then you need a plan of action. What do you want to do, what service or services do you want to provide, how much will it cost, where will you run from, do you want to run it yourself or do you want something more structured? There are many questions you need to ask yourself before an idea can move towards becoming a reality.

Your local Community Volunteering Service can be a big help in answering some of the above questions, each town will have one and their advice is usually free. If you have no CVS then go to the Citizens Advice Bureau who may be able to advise you. Whatever it is you want to do it's best' right from day one' to start to make contacts with organisations that can help you. Whether that help be advice or financial assistance. Most voluntary work is not about money.

If you are going to need money to get your idea off the ground then there are a few things you need to be aware of. Firstly if you wish to run something on your own, as a social enterprise, then in my experience you need to be aware that there will be precious few doors open to you for finance, to get money for your project you need a steering group or committee and a constitution.

These were the issues I faced when Trans-Shropshire started off. It was almost impossible to get funding running it as a social enterprise, though my local council was supportive and a small grant from Unltd* (a type of lottery grant) was awarded to me.

Within a year of starting, we formed a committee and adopted a constitution. A constitution is basically a set of aims and guidelines for running your group, the Charity Commission provides an excellent base document if this is the road you want to travel.

If you do not want to become that formal and only want to set up something that loosely structures the group, then a steering group is an option. With a steering group you can still adopt a constitution but it does not have to be too formal, merely a list of aims and objectives that the group wants to follow, this is often sufficient for some funding to be obtained.

When I was involved with the Telford Gay Group, running a local LGBT. friendly entertainment evening, once a week, this was the route we chose to follow and it worked well. We had a core group of three, Chair, Treasurer and Secretary and a general steering group that advised us on the needs of the community. All decisions were ultimately taken by the core group but the general steering group spoke for the community.

When I was involved with Woman to Woman providing support to women who were questioning their sexuality, we had a very informal structure of a steering group with a simple, one page, constitution. However this was enough for us to get an 'Awards for All' lottery grant to keep us afloat and pay the overheads of running the group.

It is not complex setting up a service of some kind on a voluntary basis as long as you understand what it is you want to do, the service you want to provide and how to get funding for your project. I hope the previous information will assist you if this is something you wish to do.

Currently I am working approximately 35hrs+ a week as a volunteer and find it very challenging at times. There have been weeks when I seem to do nothing but volunteer and my work – life balance goes out of the window.

Clearly it is unhealthy to lose balance in any career we have, at all times we must care for ourselves first otherwise we have nothing to give to other people.

Work, rest and play. Eat well, sleep well and give stress the heave ho. If we keep to this simple plan for our own mental health and well being we can, in return, help others to do something about their own lives, through voluntary work or paid work.

A couple of last thoughts on volunteering.

I feel we must always remember that it is not our place to tell someone what to do; people should always retain and make their own choices. If we provide a friendly, non judgmental and inclusive atmosphere then people will come and support your work or want to use the facility you provide.

When things go wrong, which often they do, try not to take it personally. We are only human and can only do our best to try and help other people.

On the odd occasion someone has been unhappy with the service that they have been provided via one of the projects I have been involved in. I had always in the past, taken it personally because I have tended to put too much of myself into what ever it is I am involved in.

This was not healthy for me or them and I needed a big lesson in setting boundaries for myself. The training I received to become a counsellor helped me understand what this was about and to set boundaries appropriate to the work I do.

Sometimes we just have to accept that not everything is within our control and to let it go.

Easy said – hard to do.

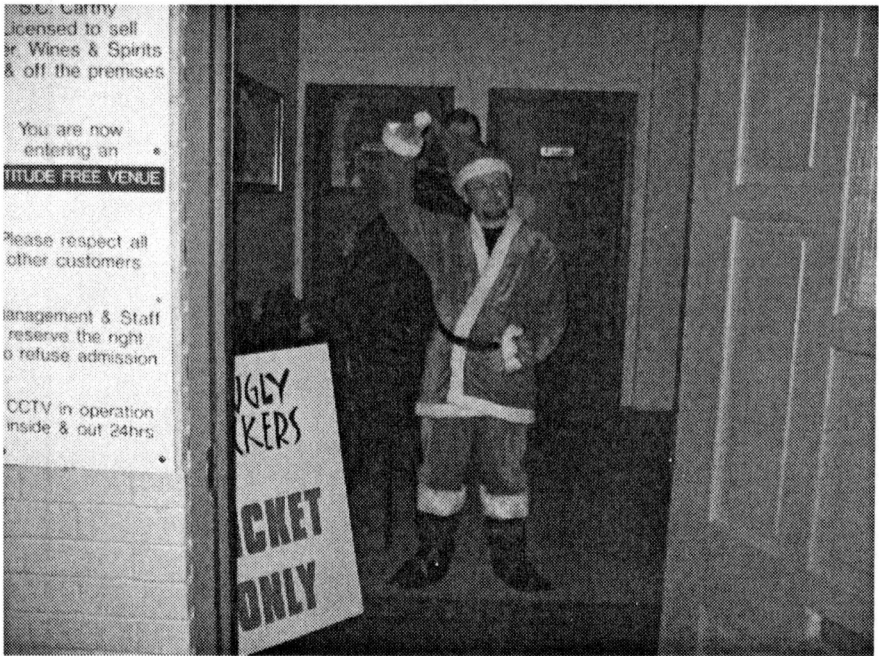

Volunteering can be fun: Trans-Shropshire Christmas Party 2004

The Infamous 5 - Telford's own "Very Haunted Team", raising the profile of
Trans-Shropshire & the Gender Advisory Bureau with a ghost hunting fund-raiser.

T R A N S M A N

In Conclusion

IF YOU ARE READING THIS chapter I am going to assume that you have read the rest of the book first. I know not everybody does but it helps me to persevere if I think you have read it, after all I am not doing this for the sake of wasting time. The point is to try and raise awareness around trans issues and I have made a choice to use my own story to do just that.

Believe me, it was not an easy decision to put pen to paper and discuss openly all the ins and outs of my life including all the intimate details of my sex life! What was even harder was to include personal pictures in this book. By publishing the pictures of who I was and who I have become has opened me up to many a comment that will not necessarily be on the good side.

I believe that people are very visual and reading lots of words does not always convey the message across. Pictures give reality to a story, depth to the character and engage the reader more fully in the process of digesting whatever message is within the text.

I have put pictures of my childhood and my adult life, as well as pictures of some of the surgery I chose to have. From these I hope you can see that I was for all purposes a woman in the eyes of society and further, that surgery is no 'soft' option, it is a challenging time for all those who tread that path.

When I was 18 years old I registered with a modelling agency and secured work as an artist's model with some photographic work too.

Though at 4ft 11 I was not the best for photographic modelling, much to my annoyance at the time.

Photo sent to register at 'Joy Belles Modelling Agency' (Aged 18)

I remember my mother being distraught when I came home and said I was starting at the Wakeman School of Art in Shrewsbury as an artist's model. She felt it was the worst thing I could have done to her except perhaps, be a prostitute and said how could she ever hold her head up again in the little town where we lived,.

I entered beauty competitions namely Miss Shropshire and Miss Butlins, and came 2nd or 3rd. It would have been nice to come first but hey, shit happens, the point I am trying to make is that clearly I was a feminine female.

I married twice and had four wonderful children, the truth is I would have had a damn sight more of them if I had been able to carry the pregnancies to term. I had a good home and loving husbands and I know that both men did their best to love me and provide for me. I was an upstanding member of the local community and devoutly religious, I taught the bible to many people and firmly believed, at that time, the truths I was teaching. In short I was, as I said previously, a woman in the eyes of society, the last person on earth anyone would have considered to be transsexual.

When I find myself delivering training to professionals on GID. there is this assumption that transmen like myself come from the lesbian community. That they are some kind of masculinised lesbian who wants to take that next step, namely hormones and or surgery, to mimic men.

The reality is that some lesbian women have a really hard time trying to accept me and I am sure that I am not alone with some other transman in feeling the effects of conflict. Some of the strongest threats, verbal and physical, have been from women who identify as lesbian and see me as some kind of traitor to the cause or threat on their territory.

I did not come from the lesbian community, though I did spend some time being identified as lesbian by others who did not understand how I felt about myself. I was no 'butch' lesbian, no I was for all purposes a woman and very feminine, having everything in my hand that any woman could possibly want, but I was unhappy and was not prepared to stay in a life that would leave me full of regrets in my old age.

I have to acknowledge that I hurt a lot of people in my life, in my struggle to break out of the shell of womanhood and for that I am truly sorry but in all honesty I have no regrets. I would do the same tomorrow if I had to live my life over again.

I am often asked if I feel I should have transitioned earlier in my life rather than in my mid thirties and this is a very good question. I believe that I would not have been able to transition earlier in my life. I believe it was maturity itself that helped me to understand who and what I was, maturity gave me the stability to transition with balance.

I feel that my life is rich and all the richer for having lived it as a woman for 30+ years. Who I was, is who I am now, simply the outside has changed to fall inline with how I feel on the inside. People tell me all the time that I have changed and am not the person they used to know but is this really true?

Is it not more likely that because they now see me as male they are seeing all that I am and do so in a different way?

I still have the same values, abilities, family loyalties, annoying health problems, and more. I am not somebody different to the person they knew for 30 odd years, my outside is different yes, my name is different, but me the person is still the same. If I was their friend before I am still now, I am still my brother and sisters sibling, I am still the parent of my children, I am still the child of my parents, all our shared memories still exist.

I often have it asked of me that if society was more accepting of difference would I have felt the need to transition at all, could I not have lived as a male without surgery if people had been less judgmental?

In conclusion I would have to say that whether society accepted me or not living as a man, my female body became an abhorrence to me and it had to go.

The future may bring a time when society is more accepting of people who have variant gender identities but this does not mean we would not want to take hormones and surgically alter our bodies.

This is not about society, this is about us, who we are underneath our skin, what we see in the mirror.

In all honesty I can never see a time, even if society makes that great leap of acceptance of all difference, when people like me will no longer exist. For as long as there are people who by a quirk of biology are born with a brain contrary to their biological state

Men and Women of transsexual origin will come forward for treatment.

I firmly believe that treatment should be available to all those who, after careful consideration and education on the implications of the choice they are making, still wish to transition into what they believe to be their true gender. For many this treatment simply is the difference between life and death.

I for one will continue to do my bit to try and educate the 'powers that be' in my little corner of rural England, on who we are and what we want and after reading this book I hope you feel the same.

Thank you for staying with me and hope I you enjoyed the journey.

Footnote: Whilst preparing this manuscript for publication I received my Gender Recognition Certificate through the post, acknowledging me as male and allowing me to now marry the woman that I love. Interestingly the certificate arrived on my birthday, 43 years to the day I was born and the error of recording me as female had occurred. Spooky, fluky and possibly fate, but a fitting end to this book as the new chapter in my life begins.

Life goes on; photo's from Majorca December 2004

Further places to obtain information on Transsexualism.

I would like to point out that the service providers listed below are only **a selection** of the overall number of organisations within the UK.

I have listed those service providers that I used myself when 'coming out' as trans and those, namely Trans-Shropshire and the G.A.B, that I have been directly involved in.

Gender Advisory Bureau.

Diversity & Equalities training provider to public services in the UK

The Gender Advisory Bureau has been set up, in the light of the Gender Recognition Act, as a "Not for Profit" business to deliver affordable and effective training to public service providers anywhere it is needed in mainland UK.

The G.A.B. runs regular monthly seminars, half day/full days training and Corporate options. They will also provide consultancy on equalities policies etc.

Phone 01952 253578 or 253577   Email g.a.b@btconnect.com

Trans-Shropshire.

A registered charity number 1110042 covering the West Midlands and surrounding areas (UK). Providing a range of services for trans persons and their families.

Trans-Shropshire run a five morning a week drop-in facility, specialist counselling services, reference library, social groups, regular social events and more.

www.trans-shropshire.org.uk

Phone 01952 240099   Email info@trans-shropshire.org.uk

Gender Identity Research and Education Society (GIRES).

This registered charity produces a wide range of literature, aimed at different audiences. A list of its publications can be obtained from its website: http://www.gires.org.uk, or by telephoning 01372 801554.

www.gires.org.uk

Press for Change

Press for Change is a political lobbying and educational organisation, which campaigns to achieve equal civil rights and liberties for all transgender people in the United Kingdom, through legislation and social change.

Email www.pfc.org.uk

Gender Trust

A registered charity providing a range of services to trans persons in the UK

The objective of the Gender Trust are:

To relieve the mental and emotional stress of all persons who are in any manner affected by Gender Dysphoria related to Transgenderism and Transsexualism; particularly to protect the good mental and physical health of all such persons.

To advance public education about all the aspects of Gender Dysphoria related to Transgenderism, Transsexualism.

www.gendertrust.org.uk

FTM network

About the FTM Network

The FTM network is an informal and Ad hoc self help group, open to all female to male transgender and transsexual people, or those exploring this aspect of their gender. Currently it has over 750 members in Britain and Europe, and contact with F to M groups in America, Belgium, France, Russia, China, Japan and Australia

Website: www.ftm.org.uk

A selection of interesting books to read other than the wealth of leaflets that are available from all of the above named support groups, would be:

Sex Gender & Sexuality by Tracy O'Keefe ISBN 0952948222

Man into Woman – The First Sex Change by Neils Hoyer ISBN 0954707206

Conundrum by Jan Morris ISBN 057120946-7

FTM Transsexuals in Society by Holly Denor ISBN 0253212596

Transsexed and Transgender People – A Guide. Gendys by Alice Purnell ISBN 0952510774

Printed in the United Kingdom
by Lightning Source UK Ltd.
116274UKS00001B/345